JUSTICE
on
EARTH

◆

PEOPLE OF FAITH WORKING AT THE INTERSECTIONS OF RACE, CLASS, AND THE ENVIRONMENT

Manish Mishra–Marzetti and
Jennifer Nordstrom

EDITORS

Skinner House Books

BOSTON

www.skinnerhouse.org

Printed in the United States

Text design by Jeff Miller.

print ISBN: 978-1-55896-813-4
eBook ISBN: 978-1-55896-814-1

6 5 4 3 2
21 20 19 18

Library of Congress Cataloging-in-Publication Data
Names: Mishra-Marzetti, Manish, editor.
Title: Justice on earth : people of faith working at the intersections of
    race, class, and the environment / Manish Mishra-Marzetti and Jennifer
    Nordstrom, editors.
Description: Boston : Skinner House Books, 2018. | Includes bibliographical
    references. |
Identifiers: LCCN 2017043727 (print) | LCCN 2017048340 (ebook) |
    ISBN 9781558968141 () | ISBN 9781558968134 (pbk. : alk. paper)
Subjects: LCSH: Religion and justice.
Classification: LCC BL65.J87 (ebook) | LCC BL65.J87 J868 2018 (print) |
    DDC 261.8--dc23
LC record available at https://lccn.loc.gov/2017043727

We gratefully acknowledge permission to reprint the following: "I don't know
what sort of a God . . ." from *Kabir: Ecstatic Poems by Robert Bly*, copyright ©
2004 by Robert Bly, reprinted by permission of Beacon Press, Boston; an
excerpt from "Fossil Fuel" by John Dickson, reprinted by permission of the
author's estate.

Contents

MANISH MISHRA−MARZETTI

❖

Introduction

In the fall of 2013, I received an unusual invitation from the Unitarian Universalist Ministry for Earth (UUMFE). It was an invitation to attend something the organizers were billing as a "Collaboratory" (a collaborative laboratory) in Detroit the following March. I was a bit perplexed. While I have always cared about the environment, I would not have called myself an environmentalist. Within Unitarian Universalism, I have been a leader in our people of color community and a proponent of issues related to racial, cultural, and ethnic diversity. None of my work within Unitarian Universalism to date had been related to environmentalism, and so I was left wondering why UUMFE was extending this invitation to me.

As it was explained to me, UUMFE had recognized that it wanted to build bridges with activists from other communities and explore how we might all come together in ways that are collaborative and mutually supportive. This sounded fine to me. In all honesty, it helped that I had extended family in the metro Detroit area. I wasn't sure about this "Collaboratory" business, but if it was just another think-tank session at least I had relatives that I could look forward to catching up with afterward. So I accepted the invitation.

There are times when we experience unexpected grace in our lives, and those months of early 2014 stand out as such a time for me, for multiple reasons. As an adoptive parent, you never know when the timing of a potential adoption might work out, and in February of that year our newborn daughter joined our family. Both she and her older brother are African American. Just weeks after she became a part of my life, I journeyed to Detroit, which I came to discover is a city that starkly highlights the difficulties and challenges facing many minorities living in our urban centers. I thought I was traveling to Detroit to participate in a think tank, but it was so much deeper and more profound than that: It was an experiential learning, justice-oriented, innovative, and intentionally bridge-building journey that left an indelible imprint on my soul.

That experience in Detroit was, for me, a primer on America's troubled and complicated history with urban minority populations. Like many cities across the American landscape, Detroit lost well-paying manufacturing jobs in the 1960s and 1970s. Simultaneously, with civil rights groups pressing for racial integration in schools, housing, and other settings, many Caucasian Americans began moving to the suburbs. With the economic collapse came the crash of residential housing markets in Detroit and many other cities; middle-class housing suddenly became "affordable housing," thereby attracting populations with more limited financial means—typically African-American and Latinx communities. Several other developments occurred at the same time. Because funding for public schools is typically tied to residential housing prices, the financial base for many urban school districts also collapsed. And, as these once middle- to upper middle-class communities became lower-income, non-white communities, they also lost economic and political influence.

Across the United States, this phenomenon has taken place in other major urban centers over and over again, with the exact same results: As white middle-class populations abandoned the urban setting, minority and poorer populations became the dominant groups. But, as the Collaboratory helped bring alive, the story didn't end there. As these urban centers became impoverished communities with relatively less political clout, policy decisions were made in ensuing decades that led to poor and non-white communities becoming the destination for the waste and pollution of more affluent, typically white, communities. Locating power plants, waste facilities, and pollution-generating industries in minority and lower-income settings became the national norm. This further depressed housing prices in those areas, creating a whole new set of additional problems: illnesses related to pollutants, troubles with water quality, and a rise in cancer and childhood asthma rates, among others. In the decades since the collapse of urban manufacturing, we, as a nation, have taken an already difficult socioeconomic situation and made it worse.

I knew about all of this on some unspoken, subconscious level. As Americans, we're not supposed to talk about the fact that our middle class may be built on the backs of our poor and Brown and Black folks. But to experience this reality firsthand—to be in Detroit, standing on the sidewalk as a garbage truck from Grosse Pointe, an affluent community approximately fifteen miles away, pulls in to drop off its trash in an African-American and Latinx neighborhood—left my heart in deep pain. As a society, we have learned to turn a blind eye to the racialized, highly oppressive, and reinforcing cycles of poverty in these urban zones. Standing in the parking lot of a public elementary school, the student body of which is 90 percent African American, smelling the fumes from the incinerator situated next door, is enough to bring tears to one's eyes.

This is what made the UUMFE's Collaboratory so effective; it was experiential learning at its best. Not only did it bring us physically into the urban context of Detroit, but it also placed us in direct dialogue with local residents and leaders. This was not academic, textbook learning, but rather face-to-face social learning in a context that we were studying and experiencing firsthand. What became increasingly clear over the course of our experience in Detroit is that the issues we were encountering were all profoundly linked: Lack of economic opportunity is tied to the quality of local schools and the health impacts of pollution; the inability to access clean water and healthy food directly impacts one's ability to function in school or at work; and the intentional siting of power plants and waste facilities away from wealthier and whiter communities impacts local housing prices, affects health, and points toward endemic, structural racism. It is all linked; no single piece stands in isolation. Just as importantly, these insights are not only about Detroit—they are about how we understand and work toward justice, wherever we are.

The value of bringing an intersectional lens to justice-making work was a profound realization for me, and it was exactly the point that the UUMFE was trying to make via the Collaboratory and by inviting me, a self-proclaimed non-environmentalist, into their circle. I found myself so deeply affected by the need for intersectional justice-making that I volunteered on the spot to help bring this book to press. This is a book about environmental justice, yes, but it is also much more than that. It holds subtly within its pages a prayer for greater unity, collaboration, and mutual support in all the justice work we do. I hope and trust that you may read it with that prayer in mind, reflecting on how an intersectional approach toward justice-making might be unifying, impactful, and spiritually transformative.

JENNIFER NORDSTROM

❖

Intersectionality, Faith, and Environmental Justice

I N 2010, a group of young adults gathered for Disarmament Summer in Chimayo, New Mexico, just down the
road from Los Alamos National Nuclear Weapons Laboratory.
We called ourselves Think Outside the Bomb, and we were
White, Chicano, Indigenous, Black, Latinx, and more. We had
been invited there by a leader in the Tewa tribe, on whose
land the lab sits, and we were there to protest nuclear weapons, nuclear energy, uranium mining, and militarism. We held
a ten-day direct action and permaculture training camp, which
culminated in a beautiful, puppet-filled community protest
at the nuclear weapons lab. We wanted to build resistance to
white supremacy and militarism. We also wanted to build an
alternative vision of the world that was environmentally sustainable and socially just. We learned how to grow food, build
sustainable life systems, and cultivate cross-cultural relationships of equality and respect. For us, these were not separate
issues. They were inextricably related to each other, multiple
parts of the same whole.

In 1989, author, scholar, and critical race theorist Kimberlé Williams Crenshaw introduced the term *intersectionality* to describe the way societal patterns of power and oppression overlap and intersect with one another. Crenshaw explained that broad systems of power like white supremacy, patriarchy, and capitalism are fundamentally related, and they interact through patterns in society. When these patterns of power intersect, they affect each other's particular manifestation of the larger overarching pattern of that moment in history. For instance, when patterns of colonialism, white supremacy, and capitalism intersected, they created a new system of chattel slavery, which produced a long-term system of slave labor in the United States based on constructed ideas of racial difference.

Patterns of power intersect in the lives, bodies, and experience of individuals as well as in broader society. Individuals experience patterns of power differently depending on where and how the larger forces overlap in their lives. For example, women will experience sexism differently depending on their race, class, gender identity, and sexuality. People of color will experience racism differently based on their class, gender, gender identity, and sexuality. Those overlapping and intersecting patterns of power affect people differently depending on their context. We must consider, for instance, where and when race and class are intersecting and *the environment in which they intersect* at a given moment.

In my experience as an organizer and a professional, I have found that bringing in additional knowledge from other fields, other issues of concern, and other understandings of patterns of power and oppression has strengthened the work. Single-issue silos of concern that don't account for the overlapping intersection of patterns of power result in narrower understandings of their own issue. They miss complexity, and often fail to build effective partnerships with diverse communities affected by the issue because they don't understand the complex ways in which various communities are affected. This book notices that tendency in Unitarian Universalist responses to justice issues and attempts to begin a dialogue about intersectionality, proposing the frame of environmental justice as one avenue to a more holistic approach to our justice work, our eschatology, and our lives.

Throughout this book, you will find Unitarian Universalist authors exploring how the theoretical concept of intersectionality and the framework of environmental justice can broaden and deepen Unitarian Universalist theory and practice. They also provide opportunities for more holistic, accountable, and connected justice efforts. Several of the essays unpack particular aspects of intersectionality and environmental justice, including the history of the environmental justice movement in the United States; how various theologies informed by intersectionality and environmental justice can dialogue with UU theologies; and how a responsible and accountable ethic of environmental justice reckons with UU theological history. The essays also describe how practicing intersectionality could change Unitarian Universalism and how intersectionality offers a vision for justice work that honors diverse and complex relationships to the whole.

I first learned about environmental justice from the communities of color that partnered with Think Outside the
Bomb. Most of our primary partners were other youth and
young adults, including Indigenous young adults from the
Multicultural Alliance for a Safe Environment, Chicano youth
and young adults from the Products of Atzlan, and a national
coalition of youth and young adults of color called Building
Action for a Sustainable Environment (BASE). These partners
taught us about how communities of color were exploited
and poisoned through the entire nuclear fuel cycle: from
uranium mining on Indigenous lands to nuclear weapons
production on Indigenous land and the contamination of
surrounding Indigenous, Chicano, and Latinx communities
to nuclear waste storage in communities of color. These environmental justice organizations highlighted the relationships
between militarism, colonialism, racism, and the environment.

Prior to that summer I had considered myself an environmentalist, but it had not been the primary identifier in my
life. It was one piece of my larger commitment to a more just,
more beautiful, and life-sustaining world. But I had thought
of the environment as something separate from humans—
trees, water, and the earth. I had not made a connection
between the environment and the various communities of
people that live in it. I learned from environmental justice
organizations led by people of color that the environment
includes everything around us: nonhuman nature, the streets,
people, patterns of oppression, differing experiences of the
environment mitigated by those patterns, *as well as* trees, water,

and the earth. When I move through spaces, I do so as a whole person with varying identities. Those spaces are "the environment," and they are run through by patterns of power and oppression as much as they are filled with roads, trees, industries, air, water, and other people. My experience of those spaces is mitigated by how my identities interact with power constructs.

Contrary to some understandings of environmentalism—including many Unitarian Universalist framings—the environment is not simply natural wilderness in need of saving. Indeed, that understanding is grounded in colonialism and white supremacy. When we imagine a single type of natural environment, and a single human experience of that environment, we collapse diverse and complex human experiences and erase intricate patterns of power and oppression. Unitarian Universalism must confront our historical and contemporary construction of theologies that have participated in this erasure, as noted by essayist Sophia Betancourt. There is not a single experience of the environment divorced from other relationships, or a single experience of humanity divorced from the environment. Rather, a variety of experiences are influenced by overarching patterns in society and they intersect with each other, humans, and nonhuman nature.

When we focus our justice work on a single type of experience without an intersectional analysis, we limit ourselves and other people from living whole and connected lives. We limit our ability to experience our own whole being and that of others. We do not engage with the full reality of the world.

We cut ourselves and others off from the diversity of human experience and the varieties of knowledge in the world. Intersectional analysis brings us in contact with broader and deeper understandings of the world.

When we do justice work in silos, we only focus on a single aspect of justice, which is not true to our whole lives, or to the wholeness of other people. When single-issue justice work lacks an intersectional analysis, it usually caters to the dominant identities within the issue. For instance, while the entire world is threatened by climate change, the individual threats we face as a result of it are particular to where we live and our access to power and resources. People in formerly colonized countries, who have experienced fewer benefits of the industrialization that has caused climate change, are more likely to experience harm from climate change sooner, and with fewer resources to adapt and survive. In addition, the process of industrialization included the theft of colonized peoples' resources, while colonization simultaneously wreaked havoc on cultures, people, and land. When we do not recognize overlapping and interacting patterns of power and oppression and their effects on peoples' lives, we collapse experience into dominant narratives and erase histories and bodies. Thus, we support the dominant sides of the power axes of all the issues not being considered in the single-issue silo.

In addition to intersectionality, the second resource for powerful environmental justice work that we explore in this book is faith. Several essays explore how we might do intersectional work for environmental justice as *faith* work— specifically, how our faith as Unitarian Universalists can ground and nurture our work for environmental justice. My own work for justice is grounded in my faith—in my deep love for humanity, nonhuman beings, and the earth. The core of my being is connected to the larger systems of life, and I feel them tug at me to be part of moving my own life, my community, and humanity back toward right relationship. This tug, this call of the deep to the well of my own soul, is what brings me back to justice work when I am tired, bored, or despairing.

Over the years, I have found that in order to continue the work I need to return to my source—love and commitment to life, no matter the result. My faith inspires and grounds my work for justice, and it cannot be separated from that work any more than the pieces of my identity can be separated from one another. When I have tried to separate my justice work from my faith, I have burned out and caused harm to myself and others. This book aims to provide resources to create and sustain a connection between your faith and environmental justice work. Without the call of interconnection, I would not have the motivation to do intersectional justice work. Without the experience of interconnection, I would not have the energy or stamina to continue it. There were Disarmament Summer days when the size and power of our opponent—the cornerstone of the United States military—were so overwhelming that I felt foolish. There were days when I felt so deeply the devastation of the communities I was living in and working with that I teetered on the edge of despair.

The promise and threat of justice work in a community you love is that it goes deep into your being. It can make you feel like your life is worth living, that you are part of life flourishing, part of something bigger than yourself that matters to the whole. It can also make you feel despair about your own life and the future of humanity and the earth. The stakes are high and the work is treacherous. It can feel like walking on a mountain ridge in the fog with lives depending on arriving safely at our destination. We are not sure when we will get there or how, but we know we must. The final four essays in this book are practical examples of this high-ridge walking, written by authors who have done intersectional environmental justice work in faith communities.

I have lived my life as a border-walker, between identities, communities, and fields of knowledge. I still need religious community in order to do the justice work well. We do the work together so we can encourage each other and help each other watch out for cliffs and boulders. We learn how to share the task, recognizing that our intersectional analysis is bolstered by people who experience the world through different identities. We help each other understand the world and our varied perceptions of it. Together, we will have a more holistic understanding of patterns of power and oppression and how they affect our intersectional work for justice. We also help each other return to our deepest values and highest resolve when we fall into our own habitual failings. We return to spiritual practice for resilience, nourishment, and integrity. We encourage each other toward and hold each other accountable to the whole and to the vision of Beloved Community for which we work.

TAKING IT FURTHER

Watch Kimberlé Crenshaw's Keynote address to the Women of the World Festival 2016, in which she gives an "Intersectionality 101" introduction to the concept she coined in 1989.

. . . . .

What overlapping patterns of power and oppression have you experienced in your own life? How have they manifested in the institutions in which you live and work? How have they affected your experience of your own identity?

. . . . .

Are there any environmental justice organizations active in your community? Go to one of their events and learn from them.

PAULA COLE JONES

❖

The Formation of the
Environmental Justice Movement

I N 2014 a small group of people from around the country
assembled for an environmental justice Collaboratory to
reimagine the future of environmental work in the Unitarian
Universalist Association. The planners wisely chose to gather
in Detroit and arranged for us to visit with local environmental activists. This city in decline has suffered from loss of
industry, loss of people as the jobs left, and the reduction of
municipal services. On the surface, one sees a city landscape
dominated by abandoned homes, crumbling industrial plants,
and sparsely traveled streets. But tucked away in neighborhoods are schools, community gardens, and coalitions of
people working on local issues. We met with people who
are fighting for access to municipal water services and the
enforcement of clean air standards at recycling plants. We saw
operations for equipping and engaging citizens in urban agriculture to meet the city's goal of food sovereignty. We dined at
establishments that use locally grown produce and train people
for jobs in the food and hospitality industries. Consistent

among the different groups we spoke with was their value for life in the community, sustainable lifestyles, and clear self-determination. Detroit was a good backdrop for conversations about the environment, economics, racial equality, governance, and justice. One thing I heard in this progressive community that I haven't forgotten is the statement, "No one is expendable. Everyone matters."

When "We the People" organize to amplify our voices, our power, and the demand for justice, we call on our democracy to work. Movements awaken people to our shared humanity and perils by highlighting problems and demanding change of the people who hold the power to make decisions. These decision-makers are often those elected or hired to serve the public. The people become a part of the apparatus that shapes public agendas and they help to redefine aspects of culture and improve conditions for citizens. We all learned this from the lessons of the civil rights movement, which was an important precursor to the environmental justice movement. African Americans and allies persistently and strategically organized to strengthen the demand for equal rights in the United States. As they did, they awakened a nation and the world to the disgrace of racial discrimination and injustice. Brutal violence, inflicted by the state and white citizens against peaceful demonstrators who sought to change policies and practices that sanctioned racial segregation and discrimination and excluded African Americans from mainstream society, was bared for all to see. And while the passage of the 1964 Civil Rights Act included language guaranteeing "protection from discrimination based on race, color, religion, sex, or national origin," it did not undo an entrenched national history of structured inequality and racial bias. Racism was still in place and needed to be addressed.

It has long been understood that unpopular environmental decisions often follow the "path of least resistance," but we should expand this assertion to include the path of structured or institutional discrimination. To say that decisions follow the path of least resistance takes the focus off of the systemic nature of oppression; specifically, who gets to make the decisions. There are many examples of communities of color and low-income communities that are at risk due to pollution from the placement of industrial sites, environmental waste disposal, resource retrieval or use, and air and water pollution. These communities often bear the negative historical impact of racial and ethnic segregation, income inequality, and limited access to resources and policy makers. They also often benefit the least from state and corporate decisions and practices that lead to environmental degradation, make communities and dwellings unsafe, and result in health problems, losses in quality of life, and lower property values.

A few historical reference points help to explain what makes the environmental justice movement unique. The worst national environmental crisis was the Dust Bowl in the 1930s. The combination of land clearing, overgrazing cattle, and severe drought was a perfect storm that plunged the country into the Great Depression. People left unproductive rural communities and migrated to cities looking for food and work. Unemployment and poverty soared. President Franklin D. Roosevelt's administration passed the New Deal, creating federal infrastructure and resources that provided technical, financial, and legislative support to prevent similar occurrences in the future. The New Deal provided resources for renewing the land and putting people back to work. There was a great deal of environmental activity across the country, including the creation of the Civil Conservation Corps, which repaired waterways, paved roads, planted trees for windbreaks, and built state parks. In her paper "Dust Bowl Meets Great Depression," Eliza Williams observes that the modern environmental movement could have followed the Dust Bowl, but the Great Depression made it impossible. This period of restoring the environment preceded the modern environmental movement, which happened at a time of great prosperity.

World War II brought the Great Depression to an end. The US economy recovered, as industry production and civilian employment increased to meet the new demands. After the war ended in 1945, the United States saw a huge boom in housing, automobile manufacturing, and other industries. From 1945 to 1960, a rapidly growing post-war economy coupled with increased production, increasing waste and producing massive environmental pollution. The lack of industrial regulation took a toll on the environment, wildlife, and some local communities. Widespread public concern about pollution was triggered by the 1962 publication of Rachel Carson's book *Silent Spring*. Citizens and government officials started paying attention to Carson's warnings about the dangers of the pesticide DDT and other chemicals that were poisoning the environment and becoming part of the food chain, risking the health of humans and other living things. Carson got people to see that corporate pollution was a personal issue, and she is credited with laying the foundation for the environmental movement by waking people up. President John F. Kennedy's administration began to regulate industry in order to protect the environment.

The modern environmental movement was a response to the economic boom experienced in the United States following World War II. It was established with the success of the first Earth Day in 1970. Earth Day was the vision of Senator Gaylord Nelson, who was bothered by the pollution he was seeing and organized states and colleges across the country to participate in a national teach-in, a valuable step in movement building. More than 20 million people participated in Earth Day on April 22, 1970. For those concerned about the environment, Earth Day became the first opportunity they had to join in a national demonstration to send a major message to public officials—to tell them to protect our planet. This groundswell of public engagement led to the establishment of the Environmental Protection Agency in 1970, enactment of the Clean Air Act of 1970, and an upgrade to the Clean Water Act in 1972, during President Richard Nixon's administration.

The environmental movement had community followers and federal support in the way of champions and institutional structure, but it had not addressed the entrenched racial inequality in the United States. It took specific organizing by people of color to prove that their communities were treated differently than white ones, leading to disproportionate health, environmental, and economic risks. The impetus for the environmental justice movement was to address environmental racism. One would need to understand the impact of racism to know why the environmental justice movement was and is necessary. In his *Sociological Inquiry* article, "Solid Waste Sites and the Black Houston Community," sociologist Robert Bullard, an early leader in the environmental justice movement, includes a 1977 quote from David Wellman: "Racism can be seen to systematically provide economic, political, psychological, and social advantages for whites at the expense of blacks and other people of color." Perhaps the environmental movement was operating from a color-blind position, assuming that race did not matter on environmental issues, especially following the Civil Rights Act, but Bullard explains why color-blindness would not bring about environmental justice: "African Americans making $50,000 to $60,000 per year are much more likely to live in a polluted environment than poor white families making just $10,000 per year." The environmental movement launched in 1970 lacked the consciousness and commitment to address structured racial and economic inequality.

The emergence of the environmental justice movement can be seen in three cases that were driven by health-related concerns of grassroots communities. The first two cases, in Niagara Falls, New York and Houston, Texas, were precursors to the movement. The third case, which occurred in Warren County, North Carolina, brought the power of the civil rights movement to the environmental conversation as a means of demanding equal rights. The New York story is well known as "Love Canal," which became national news in 1978. A small community became aware that its homes and elementary school were built on top of a hazardous waste dump. The community organizing, led by local resident Lois Gibbs, succeeded because in addition to the toxic waste surfacing on the ground and in basements, many people were sick. Women were having miscarriages and babies were born with birth defects. With help, they were able to prove that the health problems were related to the surfacing toxic wastes. Finally, they got the state and federal governments to begin correcting the problem. President Jimmy Carter designated funds to help relocate about eight hundred families. Congress passed legislation that established the Superfund, taxing petroleum and chemical companies to pay for future cleanups. It took activists from the community to demand action!

The second case was that of a middle-class African-American community in Houston that organized to prevent a waste facility from being built nearby. Attorney Linda McKeever Bullard argued the case in 1979. Her husband, the aforementioned sociologist Robert Bullard, compiled demographic information showing that eight of the ten waste sites in Houston were placed in predominantly African-American communities. Attempting to prove that race was a factor in the planned location of these waste facilities, they used Title VI of the Civil Rights Act of 1964 to argue for "protection from discrimination based on race." They did not win the case, but they did make the case for what Bullard called "a form of apartheid where whites were making decisions and black people, brown people, and people of color, including

Native Americans on reservations, had no seat at the table." This was an important case, but it did not galvanize the movement.

The environmental justice movement became nationally recognized in Warren County, North Carolina in 1982. The story spans many years, starting in 1978 with the dumping of 31,000 gallons of PCB-contaminated oil along 242 miles of highway in fourteen counties. In 1976, the Toxic Substances Control Act had been passed, requiring the cleanup of PCB spills. North Carolina's state government decided to move the contaminated soil to a landfill in a community that was the poorest in the county and the most heavily populated with African Americans. Out of concern for groundwater contamination, citizens struggled from 1978 to 1982 to prevent a permanent landfill for the toxic soil from being built. But in 1982 the government began moving 10,000 truckloads of PCB-contaminated soil to the landfill. For six weeks citizens and activists resisted and people from other parts of the country joined the organized protests. The protesters were unsuccessful in stopping the trucks. More than five hundred people were arrested, including Congressman Walter Fauntroy and pastors Benjamin Chavis (United Church of Christ) and Joseph Lowery (Southern Christian Leadership Conference), all seasoned leaders of the civil rights movement. Simultaneously, a citizen class action suit was filed. They did not win the case and or stop the landfill, but they successfully launched the environmental justice movement.

The First National People of Color Environmental Leadership Summit of 1991 brought three hundred people of color together from Native-American, Latinx, Asian-American, Pacific Islander, and African-American communities from around the United States, Puerto Rico, the Marshall Islands, and Canada. They shared stories of environmental justice issues and resulting health problems, and the group wrote seventeen Principles of Environmental Justice to frame the movement. For people of color, environmental justice is about cultural, spiritual, and physical well-being. In some cases, it is a matter of survival.

The environmental justice movement is still relatively young. The movement is active in all fifty of the United States, and in territories and countries around the world. Indicators of a growing movement can be seen in the movement's scope and influence on government policies, educational curricula, research, social studies, interdisciplinary cooperation, organization building, and the growing number of people who are concerned and engaged in protecting communities.

I was working in the US Department of Agriculture when President Clinton issued an executive order requiring agencies to provide strategic plans for environmental justice, after two attempts to pass an Environmental Justice Act failed in Congress. I was asked to facilitate the planning session for my agency. On two different occasions I sat in an auditorium in the Smithsonian Institution listening to Robert Bullard and Bunyan Bryant speak about the urgency of taking on the challenges of environmental racism. Hearing about the impact that environmental problems were having on people's lives left me thinking critically about status quo impediments to change and justice. Now, years later, with a deeper understanding of structured inequality, and the visible effects of climate change, I ask: What will it take for us to overcome racial and economic inequities and create sustainable lifestyles that restore the delicate balance between humans and nature? As Unitarian Universalists continue to work on environmentalism and climate change, we must operate with the knowledge of structured racial and economic inequality so that we are truly confronting oppression and doing our part in building the Beloved Community.

Christopher Sellers, a history professor at Stony Brook University, asks us to think of "environmental justice as a way of seeing the intersectionality of social and environmental history." Our visit to Detroit inspired us because of the intersectionality of environmental justice, food justice, racial and economic justice, governance, and voting rights.

Learn about the history of the environmental justice movement. Make this essential to your racial justice and environmental justice work. Study federal and state government environmental justice actions. Learn about who supported and who opposed environmental justice in the past. Know where community officials stand on current environmental justice issues. Discover the answers to key questions: Are environmental decisions in your community fair and equitable? Are they tied to voters' rights issues in your community? Which communities are at risk? Who is at the table? What organizations have been formed by and for people of color and working class communities to address environmental racism and classism? What cases have been fought in your community? Which ones have been won and which ones still need attention? How can you partner with people of color in your community? What are the connections between environmental justice and climate justice? Who can you invite to speak with your organization?

What can you do to build relationships, build trust, build partnerships, and make a difference?

TAKING IT FURTHER

As Paula Cole Jones suggests, we invite you to learn about local environmental justice issues. What environmental issues are nearby communities of color facing? How are legislators and other local officials engaging or not engaging in these issues? How might you and/or your community support those who are struggling with these issues?

. . . . .

Read the Environmental Protection Agency's *Eco-Justice 2020 Action Agenda* (2016), available here: https://tinyurl.com/yaabdopz.

. . . . .

Read the *Principles of Environmental Justice* written by the delegates to the First National People of Color Environmental Leadership Summit (1991), available here: ejnet.org/ej/principles.html.

SHERI PRUD'HOMME

❖

Ecotheology

A CENTURY AGO, theologians could not fathom the extent of the current ecological and social crises related to human population, industrialization, climate change, nuclear technologies, pollution, and consumption. At this moment in history the world's religions cannot escape the call to enter what scholar of religion and ecology Mary Evelyn Tucker names their "ecological phase." While ecotheologians are diverse in their particular contexts and methodological approaches, this essay—drawing significantly from ecofeminist, ecowomanist, and ecological process theology predominantly in the Christian tradition—highlights several themes in which their views constellate. The burgeoning field of ecotheology resonates with Unitarian Universalism in many regards, particularly in the interplay of the seventh and first Principles, the Sources of our faith, aspects of our theological heritage influenced by Transcendentalism, and our Universalist heritage that affirms a common destiny for all. Dialogue between Unitarian Universalist theology and ecotheology can inspire new insights for constructive ecotheologies grounded within our faith tradition. Moreover, the resonances between

Unitarian Universalist theology and ecotheology position us well to take leadership in both secular and multi-faith collaborations for environmental justice.

A prevalent theme in ecotheology is the radical interdependence of all existence and the accompanying mandate to view humankind as embedded in a complex web of relationships with other organisms that have intrinsic value. Ecotheologians arrive at this understanding from a variety of pathways. Examples include Thomas Berry and Brian Swimme's *The Universe Story*, John Cobb's relational process theology, Joanna Macy's articulation of dependent co-arising in a Buddhist cosmology, Sallie McFague's understanding of the universe as God's body, Rosemary Radford Ruether's notion of Gaia from deep ecology, and Catherine Keller's theological observations of the physics of entanglement. It is the realization that through the most basic processes of life and the universe, all that exists is in relationship with everything. As Ivone Gebara writes in *Longing for Running Water*, it "is not a mechanical interdependence but a living one: a sacred interdependence that is vibrant and visceral." A similar notion is embedded in the seventh Principle of Unitarian Universalism, "Respect for the interdependent web of all existence of which we are a part." It can also be found deeper in our theological heritage. The nineteenth-century Unitarians, especially those influenced by the Transcendentalists, saw the created world as an expression of the mind of God, each part reflecting the order and beauty of the whole. Both the Unitarians and Universalists in the nineteenth century affirmed the goodness and worth of all of creation, turning to science as an important

theological source. The theological stance of the interconnectedness of all existence is commonplace in today's Unitarian Universalist congregations. It provides a basis for
environmental justice work that includes all creatures and life
forms in the circle of moral concern, and it provides an
important counterpoint to the position that the Earth exists
solely to serve the needs and wants of humankind. It has
fueled Unitarian Universalist environmental justice initiatives
such as the 2011 "Ethical Eating: Food and Environmental
Justice" Statement of Conscience and the Commit2Respond
climate justice campaign.

A second theme weaving throughout ecotheology is God.
Most ecotheologians acknowledge that what humankind
knows about God can never be translated adequately into
words. Ivone Gebara says it well: "In the interest of broad-
ening our understanding of God, and in light of the inherent
problems that plague our traditional images of the divine, I
would dare to avoid using the word *God* so as to be able to
stammer out something about the ground of our being." In
general, ecotheologians are comfortable with an element of
mystery in conceptualizing God. As Gebara writes, "We are
always returning to this 'something more' that is both here
and there; before us, within us, and outside us; . . . transcendent and immanent; . . . spiritual and bodily—and enveloped
in *mystery*." Mystery itself can serve as a protection against the
totalizing, colonial impulse to subsume God into a narrative
that serves powers of dominance and empire, as Mayra Rivera
reminds us in her reconsideration of transcendence. In her
book *The Touch of Transcendence*, Rivera posits a relational

transcendence, "one that can resist patriarchal and imperialist assumptions while affirming not only the irreducible difference of God from all creatures, but the differences among creatures as well."

Ecotheologians have been critical of purely transcendent notions of God and the demonizing of nature, implicated in visions of an apocalyptic annihilation of this Earth. Ruether and others argue that conceptions of a neat and orderly, all-controlling, all-light, all-good, and all-powerful transcendent God serve a worldview in which the environment, women, people of darker complexion, and people of non-Christian faiths are conquered or subdued by powerful, controlling elites who elide politics, economics, and Christianity to increase their power in the name of God. As theologian James Cone puts it in his article "Whose Earth Is It Anyway?" "The logic that led to slavery and segregation in the Americas, colonization and apartheid in Africa, and the rule of white supremacy throughout the world is the same one that leads to the exploitation of animals and the ravaging of nature." In her essay "Ecology is a Sistah's Issue Too," Shamara Shantu Riley expands on the dilemma for African-American women and other people of color who have been historically associated with nature and animals as a justification for abuse, objectification, and mistreatment. She argues that rather than disassociating from nature, African-American women and other people of color along with white people need to reconceptualize race, gender, class, and nature. "If the planet as a whole is to survive," she writes, "we must all begin to see ourselves as interconnected with nonhuman nature and with one another."

Many ecotheologians agree it is no longer useful or adequate to imagine a God that existed before the cosmos, some perfect idea or being separate from all that exists who "created" life. They maintain instead that what we call God arose with our cosmos, and unfolds along with it. As Catherine Keller writes in *Face of the Deep*, "The divine and the world form the conditions of each others' becomings." In Gebara's words, "We no longer speak of God as existing before creation, but, in a way, as concomitant with it." Karen Baker-Fletcher writes in *Sisters of Dust, Sisters of Spirit*, "Creation is born out of a loving, creative dance between Spirit and the elements of the cosmos." Gebara goes on to say, "In the perspective we are developing, God is all and all is in God—including suffering, dirt, and destruction. I do not affirm the individuality of God, as the traditional perspective does, but rather God's relatedness, the understanding of which surpasses us."

God's immanence follows from such co-creative understandings of God and creation, and many ecotheologians have embraced a panentheist view. In this understanding, God is present in all of the created universe but is not identified entirely with it. As McFague explains in *The Body of God*, "Everything that is, is in God and God is in all things and yet God is not identical to the universe, for the universe is dependent on God in a way that God is not dependent on the Universe." Because God and creation participate together in the unfolding of creation, they are inextricably intertwined. For this reason, it is possible to apprehend God's presence in the natural world. Rivera affirms that "the glory of God shines in the bodies of all created beings, as a sign of their participation in God." McFague puts it this way: Everywhere we look we "would have an image of divine grandeur." Baker-Fletcher expresses a similar sentiment. She understands "God as creativity itself, with creation playing a role in God's creative activity."

As far back in our tradition as William Ellery Channing and John Murray, Unitarians and Universalists dethroned a tyrannical God that condoned violence and injustice. Theodore Parker went a step further and expanded the image of a loving Father God to include Mother. The metaphorical expansion extended into the twentieth century as evidenced in Brian Wren's hymn "Bring Many Names" in *Singing the Living Tradition*. In an understanding of the divine presence infused in all of creation, there are strong resonances with the ideas posited by Channing and developed more fully by the Transcendentalists, who turned to nature and science as ways of knowing God. In "Nature," Ralph Waldo Emerson maintained "all the uses of nature admit of being summed in one. . . . It always speaks of Spirit," for it "sees the world in God." Thomas Starr King spoke of the "gleam of the infinite majesty" that permeated all of nature.

Many twentieth-century Unitarian Universalists came to believe that while their forebears protested some of what they perceived as Christianity's errors, they did not sufficiently challenge the basic assumptions of Christian imperialism nor adequately account for evil. In many Unitarian Universalist circles, the second half of the twentieth century brought the erasure of God altogether, with the rise of religious humanism and the recognition that anthropocentric understandings of God often legitimate oppression of one group over another depending on whose image God reflects. With the rise of postmodernism at the end of the twentieth century and into the twenty-first, many Unitarian Universalist churches have experienced what one scholar has termed the "strange return of God." The UUA's 2005 Commission on Appraisal report *Engaging Our Theological Diversity* states there is a broad consensus among Unitarian Universalists that "We encounter 'God' in our own depths, in others, and in nature, seeking wholeness and transformation."

Stripped of the old anthropocentric assumptions and oppressive images, this renewed reverence and God imagery in Unitarian Universalism bears a striking resemblance to the views of many ecotheologians, and we would do well to put our theology in dialogue with their critiques and constructive proposals. It is widely recognized that communities of faith are on the forefront of many environmental justice efforts from climate change to poverty, pollution, hunger, energy use, and sustainability. Unitarian Universalists are increasingly able to participate powerfully in ecumenical and multi-faith efforts when we draw on God language and images that are inclusive, expansive, immanent, and intermingled with the unfolding of creation. Understanding the universe as a site of God's presence fuels efforts to protect and preserve the abundant diversity of creation. Understanding God as liberating and inclusive of all peoples and life forms engenders a perspective that mandates justice as much as protection and preservation. And when despair threatens to paralyze, knowing God is active in the universe's unfolding can be, for some, the difference between action and resignation.

This constellation of ideas surrounding God and creation has additional implications for the understanding of the human being. The human being in an ecotheological cosmology becomes more appropriately situated within the whole. The way Christianity has conspired with capitalism, particularly in the United States, has resulted in a culture that has erred too much on the side of individual rights, autonomy, and separateness. Moreover, it has placed humankind on the apex of a pyramid of life, privileging some humans over others as well as all humans (especially US citizens) over the rest of life in the planet's ecosystems. An ecotheological view of the human being does not compromise the particular human person as a worthwhile and valuable subject with free will and agency, deserving of dignity and respect. However, when it is understood that each person, like each living thing, is one of the diverse expressions of the multi-layered relatedness of God, then these many and multiple centers are in communion with the whole. There is no apex but rather multiple and overlapping circles. Barbara Holmes calls this aspect of the new cosmology "omnicentricity." The universe is expanding not from one point to another but from multiple points all at the same time. In *Race and the Cosmos*, she writes, "Omnicentricity means that all centers act as focal points for the activity of expansion and energy." All life forms are focal points in the cosmic dance of expansion and contraction, dependent on the physical matter of the cosmos for its very being. As Gebara puts it, "Since we are a single Sacred Body, we are within the divine, and in a certain sense we are this divinity. The individual is not annihilated, but is instead related to a wider whole without which life would be impossible." In Baker-Fletcher's words, "We humans are *adam* (which means 'earth creature' in Hebrew), dependent on all the elements of water, earth, air, sun." In this sense, there is no "immortal self" that transcends physicality. As Ruether argues in *Gaia & God*, "This concept of the 'immortal self,' survivable apart from our particular transient organism, must be recognized, not only as untenable, but as the source of much destructive behavior toward the Earth and other humans."

In this understanding, evil is not some innate quality of a fallen humanity, but wrong relationship. Human beings make choices that harm or support others in the community of life on Earth. At times, harmful choices do not even start out as cruel, but rather as the drive for life gone to excess that eclipses concern and respect for others. Ruether puts it this way: "In this sense 'good' lies in limits, a balancing of our own drive for life with the life drives of all others in which we are in community, so that the whole remains in life-sustaining harmony." Neither evil nor good is the essence of human nature, but rather a way of being and acting, the potential for which rests in all of us. In Gebara's words, "We are no longer interested in saying that human beings are good or bad by nature.... Even though we struggle against evil, we know it is part of us: it is our body, just as good, love, and mercy are." As Rita Nakashima Brock and Rebecca Ann Parker write in *Saving Paradise*, "We can come to know the world as paradise when our hearts and souls are reborn through the arduous and tender task of living rightly with one another and the earth."

Unitarian Universalism resonates with the views of these ecotheologians on the nature of human beings in the dynamic tension between our seventh and first Principles: "the interdependent web of all existence of which we are a part" and "the inherent worth and dignity of every person." Deeper in our heritage, Channing posited a relational and engaged self, tasked with unfolding the capacities of the soul in order to serve the ends of a liberating God. He saw that *imago dei* theology— affirming that human beings are made in the image of God— necessitated a responsibility to dismantle all systems or structures that would prevent life's full flourishing. This led him and many Unitarians to oppose slavery and champion other social causes. Our Universalist heritage originally affirmed a common salvation for all human souls. As both Unitarianism and Universalism have opened to the insights of scientific understandings, that notion has expanded to assert a common destiny for all life. Our Universalist heritage has caused our religious tradition to emphasize salvation resting in actions for love, healing, care, and justice in this life. Our Unitarian Universalist theological outlook, in concert with these ecotheologians, resists the impulse to separate humanity into "good guys" and "bad guys," the "pure" and "impure." Instead, it asks us as Unitarian Universalists to face the ways we are all implicated in the systems of exploitation, oppression, and destruction that we work to dismantle in our environmental justice efforts. An omnicentric and relational cosmology calls us in our environmental justice work to seek out multiple voices and multiple perspectives when considering an issue and to identify the intersections of oppressions. It also calls us to the ongoing spiritual practice of attending to the complex web of relationships in which we have our being, doing our best to live "rightly with one another and the Earth."

The role of beauty in ecofeminist theologies is the final theme, one which has been identified more frequently in the past decade. In her article "A Spirituality of Openness," Unitarian Universalist theologian Alison Downie names the power of beauty as one of the key themes present in the work of diverse Christian ecofeminist theologians. She notes that while often thought of as opposing or competing values, beauty and justice can be intimately connected. She explains that "the intertwined devastation of the Earth and dehumanizing living conditions for the most vulnerable people, often women, children, and peoples of color, are morally and aesthetically ugly. Both justice and beauty are violated when what is inherently valuable is devalued, defaced, or destroyed." Downie cautions against a simplistic understanding of beauty that one might equate with a gaze that objectifies, evaluating what is seen for utility or desirability. She also points out the qualities of openness and relationality that are central to ecofeminist theologians' understandings of the transformative power of beauty. She sees beauty in ecofeminist theology as a resource that accompanies critique and suspicion: "Attending to the power of beauty is thus not escapist; instead, it is a resource for maintaining and renewing commitment to life, grounded in gratefulness." Brock and Parker agree, "We recommit ourselves to this world as holy ground when we remember the fullness of life that is possible through our communities, our life-affirming rituals, and our love of beauty. Thus immersed, we are more responsive to and responsible for life in this world." Nineteenth-century minister theologians such as Ralph Waldo Emerson, Hosea Ballou II, and Thomas Starr King knew this well. Their legacies have passed down through the generations and are upheld in many of our congregations today in our attention to beauty in our buildings, hymns, and worship services. Our Unitarian Universalist theological heritage uniquely positions us to, as Brock and Parker put it, "enter fully—heart, mind, soul, and strength—into savoring and saving paradise."

Such attention to beauty and life-affirming commitments serves as an important counter vision to environmental justice initiatives that can burn out in their strident efforts or unintentionally disempower supporters in their apocalyptic undertones.

As Unitarian Universalist theologians and religious leaders develop religious language, symbols, and practices to inspire and sustain their congregations in the work of environmental justice, there is much to gain from dialogue with the field of ecotheology, particularly ecofeminist, ecowomanist, and process-oriented ecotheologies. The resonances with our own faith tradition are striking and reveal that we are well-situated to take leadership in environmental justice efforts. May we carry out our work for environmental justice, drawing from the aspects of our faith tradition that claim the radical interconnectedness of all existence; the mysteriousness, inclusiveness, relatedness, and immanence of God; the relatedness of the self and the ways we are called to identify and dismantle intersecting systems of oppression, violence, and destruction; and the abundant resources of beauty, love, and care that are already present and can sustain our efforts.

TAKING IT FURTHER

What is your personal theology? How does your personal theology include some of the principles that Sheri Prud'homme discusses, and in what ways is it different or distinct?

. . . . .

Prud'homme invites us to reflect on how we apply theological principles to our justice work and day-to-day lives. For example, Unitarian Universalist theologian Alison Downie reflects on the relationship between justice and beauty as principles that support ecological preservation and the sanctity of human life. How does the power of beauty affect your work for justice?

. . . . .

Ecotheologians often contend that God (the holy/sacred) is in all of the created universe and that sometimes God is creativity itself. How might thinking about God in this way support the work that you do, or could do, for environmental justice?

SOFIA BETANCOURT

❖

Ethical Implications of
Environmental Justice

"WE ARE A justice-seeking people," claims Holly Near in her song. Its presence in our hymnal and vitality when sung on marches and at rallies speaks to a central spiritual longing expressed by many Unitarian Universalists. We find ourselves called to live in solidarity with a world both claimed and characterized by injustice. Every day our tradition asks us to explore how the values we hold as sacred serve as guides in our decision making, and reminders of our accountability in impossible situations. This combination of guidance and accountability is the work of religious ethics. How we hold true to our highest ideals directly impacts the justice we pursue as a blessing to the world.

In these days when climate change rightly fills our rallying cries with notes of uncompromising urgency, we inherit a perilous tendency to sacrifice entire populations of our human family in the name of acting quickly. The path of least resistance that Paula Cole Jones addresses earlier in this collection creates "disposable" people—generally defined by class, race, ethnicity, and nation—whose particular experiences of environmental racism and injustice are erased by a movement born out of an imagined pristine wilderness empty of humanity. As Unitarian Universalists, we have a unique accountability to the ethical implications of environmental justice because we are the inheritors of religious wisdom that does not yet fully rest on the productive tension between our first and seventh Principles. We are ideally suited to engage our own religious forebears and their contributions to the environmental culture that shapes our organizing today. In so doing we can hold fast to their calls to justice (their guidance) while reimagining our connection to one another and all of nonhuman nature (our accountability).

The field of environmental ethics in a religious context often follows Aldo Leopold and Lynn White as two foundational guides for doing the difficult work of holding ourselves accountable to an Earth compromised by environmental devastation. In his 1949 landmark text *A Sand County Almanac*, Leopold builds a convincing argument for the development of what he calls a land ethic in which humanity learns to understand itself as a co-equal citizen of a land-community, rather than promoting our dominion over all of creation. The core value in the development of Earth-community and land-based environmental ethics as we know them today is rooted in his central argument: "A thing is right when it tends to preserve the integrity, stability, and beauty of the biotic community. It is wrong when it tends otherwise." Leopold draws our attention to how little emphasis is being placed on developing right relationships between humanity and the land, nonhuman animals, and plants. His focus is on how little we understand the natural world and how that ignorance undermines our ability to live out our values.

White, in contrast, attempts to understand how Western society evolved to justify profound imbalances in our relationship to Earth. He identifies the "victory of Christianity over Paganism [as] the greatest psychic revolution in the history of our culture," and condemns Christianity for its "huge burden of guilt" in justifying an unsustainable dominion as the cultural center of humanity's relationship to Earth.

These views of human superiority and the imagined right to make use of nonhuman nature as we will are faulty morals impacting the vast majority of the developed world, regardless of whether or not we subscribe to the tenets of Christianity. All too often they shield us from what would otherwise be an immense sense of outrage at the violations we have allowed. Developing an environmental ethic grounded in our desire for justice instead asks us how to develop a land ethic (or build an Earth community) in our current reimagined religious context and all that it implies.

Environmental justice pushes back on the idea that all humanity can effectively be considered as one single element of the Earth community without first dismantling generation upon generation of injustice within human society. It demonstrates how our values become blunt instruments for undoing environmental devastation when we silence the unequal consequences and risks resulting from that destruction. Instead we ask ourselves how we are called to respond to the need for a land ethic, knowing that religious culture plays a strong role in our current crisis, while simultaneously seeking justice for all people and all beings.

As Unitarian Universalists we are the inheritors of what Paul Outka calls the "Americanist environmental canon" in his groundbreaking text, *Race and Nature from Transcendentalism to the Harlem Renaissance*. We are not simply shaped by Western ideas of how our humanity relates to philosophical ideals of "nature"; we are also formed by the perspectives of foundational environmental thinkers from within our own religious tradition. We are the spiritual descendants of Ralph Waldo Emerson and Henry David Thoreau; not only are we profoundly shaped by their idealized vision of one white man communing with the wilderness, we are also responsible for reimagining the transcendence they offered us.

Situating our environmental justice work at the intersection of our first and seventh Principles demands that we address the interconnected desecration and marginalization of oppressed peoples and nonhuman nature. At the same time, we must seek understanding of what it means to be human in faithful relationship—or, we might say, in right relationship—with the rest of the Earth community. Looking to our religious forebears to better understand our historic engagement with nonhuman nature as Unitarian Universalists, it is not surprising to find that engagement more in line with what became our seventh Principle than with what became our first. The notions of inherent dignity and worth are ideals originally focused on the understanding of what it means to be fully human, and therefore address questions of humanity to the exclusion of nonhuman nature.

Human dignity and worth were not the primary environmental concerns of thinkers like Emerson and Thoreau, who were much more interested in what could be gained from an isolated communion with the natural world. Their abolitionist efforts, which are easily relatable to our first Principle, were not part of their connection to a wilderness that allows us to distance ourselves from the ugliness of everyday society in order to access a deeper truth. Consequently, we have inherited a theological vision of environmental engagement that is too often situated in a natural imaginary, a pristine landscape untrammeled and unpopulated by human beings save perhaps by the one single theologian or person of faith actively communing with a sublime part of nature. In his essay "Nature," Emerson famously calls us into solitude to gain insight and wisdom from the natural world. To free ourselves from the distractions of society, we are to "look at the stars. The rays that come from heavenly worlds, will separate between [us] and vulgar things."

Unitarian Universalists today are engaged with the work of environmental justice that seeks to repair environmental devastation while at the same time addressing gross injustices within the human family. Yet, the majority of us who live in the United States are also steeped in an environmental culture shaped by thinkers like Emerson and Thoreau. If we draw on our historic connections to both the abolition of slavery and the close connection to the natural world that is characteristic of the Americanist environmental canon, then we can choose to expand our historical quest for solitude. Our work toward environmental justice can be drawn from an intimate relationship with nature that includes, but is not limited to, the everyday interactions of our diverse human communities with nonhuman nature, one that takes seriously the unequal impacts of environmental devastation levied upon our most marginalized groups. Together, we must engage with the realities of an unjust society and lower our gaze from the stars.

In these days when Black Lives Matter claims its place as a moral imperative to follow the guidance of Black leaders and Black lives, we would do well to draw wisdom from lived experiences in the Black community. There can be no environmental ethic that centers on those most affected by environmental devastation in the United States that lacks an analysis of chattel slavery's legacy on the Black community and its relation to nonhuman nature. After centuries of forced migration, brutal violence, the stripping of agency, inhumane unpaid agricultural labor conditions, and the ongoing struggle for survival in community, a prevailing question remains whether African Americans can or should see themselves writ large as benefitting from a connection with the land. Paul Outka, a white-identified English professor specializing in African-American literature, suggests that this connection is central to the racialization of this nation as a whole and that imposed constructions of blackness and nature are the supporting pillars of white supremacy in the United States.

In *Race and Nature* Outka begins the vital, yet challenging, work of critiquing beloved founders of the US environmental movement for perhaps unwittingly colluding with nostalgic reconstructions of an imagined Southern pastoral. This is a sanitized, reconstructionist history where the land is fertile,

the enslaved are happy, and the intertwining of racialized stereotypes and the control of nonhuman nature can continue.
He contrasts our inherited, Eurocentric perceptions of the
wilderness with what he presents as a traumatic Black experience of nonhuman nature, including the historic conscription,
control, and definition of Black bodies as bestial livestock.

Here is where one white man ideally finds himself alone
in nature, in solitude, where Indigenous peoples are "removed"
from the landscape without comment or notice and all others
are ghettoized into urban wastelands to preserve for the privileged few an imaginary, untrammeled wilderness. Here is
where New England abolitionists, who are often also natural-
ists and frequently Unitarians, do not speak forcefully against
the evils of slavery until the imposition of laws such as the
Fugitive Slave Act impinge upon their own sense of liberal
freedom. Careful constructions of whiteness (and therefore of
blackness and indigeneity) depend on traditional understandings of how we experience nature. And this is vital to the
work we are called to do today. It is all too easy to erase the
wisdom of communities silenced by economic injustice, land
theft, and racism when the idea of spiritual communion with
the wilderness never once includes their presence.

This encourages the dominant assumption that communities of color in the United States are not only disengaged
from environmental concerns, or any appreciation of the natural world, but are defined by their concentration in urban
centers. It hides the insidious workings of institutional systems
of oppression that work to sustain the unearned privileges of
the dominant culture in society. It is no wonder that the

mainstream environmental movement is predominantly white, economically privileged, and frequently focused on justice for the Earth to the exclusion of all else. These patterns are born of inherited understandings and call us back to the need for intersectional theologies that can hold us accountable to multiple, interrelated truths.

We should not allow our fear or our rightful sense of immense urgency to legitimize addressing centuries of environmental devastation in isolation from centuries of human oppression and despair. Instead, we should ask ourselves what an Emersonian understanding of community can teach us about preschool classrooms filled with children of color that see toxic waste just outside their windows. We need to invite one another to imagine how to adapt Emerson's call for abolition to the needs of the present moment—while insisting that a sanitized wilderness emptied of all human life cannot offer us the wisdom we need to slow climate change or remediate climate injustice. We should take our guidance from grassroots communities working for environmental justice amid poverty and racism, and hold ourselves accountable to seeking justice for all peoples and all beings. Only then can our strivings make the Earth more whole.

TAKING IT FURTHER

Sofía Betancourt highlights the dynamic tension between Unitarian Universalism's first Principle (with its commitment to human worth and dignity) and its seventh Principle (calling for a sense of interdependence and mutuality with nonhuman nature). How do you balance and honor both of these imperatives in your spiritual life and justice work?

. . . . .

Communities of color often maintain that our societal emphasis on individualism de-emphasizes the call for mutual care and engagement that is needed in order to truly honor the dignity of all. What are your individual and/or collective relationships with communities of color? How might you reach out and deepen those relationships, from an ethic of care and mutuality?

. . . . .

Read *Race and Nature from Transcendentalism to the Harlem Renaissance* (2008) by Paul Outka.

ADAM ROBERSMITH

✧

Cherishing Our World: Avoiding Despair in Environmental Justice Work

WATCHING THE public debates about climate change is an exercise in resistance. It involves a resistance to willful ignorance; resistance to accepting all statements, especially unsubstantiated ones, as facts; resistance to the despair that can rise within us as we face the public discourse, the science, and the toll taken on human communities. Unfortunately, our individual reactions to human-caused climate change can also be unhelpful in terms of finding solutions. Some of us are panicking. Some are refusing to listen. Some are trying to scare everyone into certain behaviors (whether to reverse or ignore climate change), and others are just reporting what they think they know. With all this debate and reaction, a problem that is as large as climate change can cause paralysis, ineffectiveness, and despair.

Nevertheless, science is showing us something important: We are affecting our climate and ecosystems in ways that are detrimental to life on the planet and to how we live. We know that we need to change how we act as a species. We should have changed as a nation long ago, yet we have not. Scientists are offering research that has been confirmed repeatedly and making predictions that should frighten us all into behaving differently, yet change is not coming as many of us would expect. Research shows that our acts disproportionately affect the poor and oppressed all over the world, yet we continue to use harmful technologies and resources. It seems that simply presenting information is not enough. Scaring people with doomsday scenarios—even if they are based on our very best knowledge—does not produce sufficient change. In fact, it often creates resistance. Making pollution and waste and overconsumption sinful or shameful has some effect, but not enough to change how we behave as a culture or make policy as a nation. While these debates continue, people around the world suffer with changes they are unable to ameliorate, and those with the least power and resources suffer most of all.

This situation is not so different from one that our Universalist ancestors experienced in the 1800s. At the time, much of Christian preaching and theology was focused on hell: the burning fires and eternal torment that all would suffer if they did not fall in line with a particular set of moral ideals. Many communities of faith relied on fear to induce righteous behavior, but fear of hellfire and damnation was insufficient to eliminate undesirable behavior. If it was, sin and vice would have vanished from the American experience. It did not and has not. Hosea Ballou, a nineteenth-century Universalist who gave us some of our most basic theology and ethics, writes in *Examination of the Doctrine of Future Retribution*:

The preaching of future rewards and punishments, for the purpose of inducing people to love God and moral virtue, is not only *useless*, but *pernicious*. All such preaching, be it ever so well intended, not only amounts to a declaration, that God and moral virtue are, in themselves, unlovely, and unworthy of being loved, but, as far as it is believed, serves to alienate the affections from these most precious objects. We may illustrate this subject by the use of figures furnished in the Scriptures. There God is represented by a fountain of living waters. Divine truth, by waters, by wine and milk, by bread, etc. Should we be offered an immense reward for accepting [this nourishment], and should we be threatened with severe punishments if we refused them, it would be natural for us to suppose, that the person who should make such proposals . . . did not believe these things to be of any value in themselves . .

Ballou's theology calls us to consider our commitments and values in this day and age. Is the Earth itself without value? Are the nourishments, life-sustaining cycles, and blessings of this world only worth saving because we should be afraid of some hellish future? Our climate discourse has failed because we as a people have not understood the real value of our environment. Our environment is not valuable because it has a financial equivalent. It is not valuable because scientists and some activists tell us that if we do not stop sinning against the Earth (over-consuming fossil fuels, for example), we will create an apocalypse. The Earth is valuable because it is good and is a dynamic, living ecosystem. If people, creatures of this Earth, have worth and dignity, we must recognize that the Earth itself, the home and origin of those creatures, has worth and dignity as well. If we, as a nation, a people, or a species, loved this planet as our Universalist ancestors understood loving God, we would have already made so many different choices about how we live on this Earth and with each other.

Imagine how we might engage with one another and the environment if we held to this extension of Ballou's theology. We would look at the environmental impact of mountaintop removal or strip mining as a great harm to be stopped, regardless of whether the communities near the mine were wealthy or poor. We would understand that poisoning water with pollutants was unacceptable whether it supplied an urban center, a Native American reservation, a tourist destination, or a national park. We would understand that if climate change makes inhabited spaces uninhabitable for humans, plants, or animals, then we should avoid it at all costs because it degrades what is good. Our choices, policies, and economics would no longer be based on the premise that harming those with the least power inflicted the least harm. Instead, we would see that environmental injustice exponentially increases the harm by allowing damage to those people and things we should be most careful to protect.

In looking at the different ways people respond to the concepts of climate change, ecological damage, and environmental injustice, we can see that much of it is a reaction to fear: fear of having to change how we think about the world and our lives, fear of catastrophe, fear of responsibility for actions and choices. Yet, fear is not an effective motivator—it creates paralysis. It feeds into the kind of despair that says, Well, I cannot do anything about it anyway and doom is coming, so I'll just keep on as I am. Hell is inevitable, since I cannot be good enough. The seas will rise and the Earth turn to desert—people will drown here and starve there—because I cannot change everything.

Ballou counsels us further:

> All who preach the doctrine of future punishment, have relied on the terrors of that punishment to induce [people] to be pious and virtuous; and yet they know that the most vicious and most abominable in all Christian countries, have been brought up from childhood to believe that doctrine; and at the same time have been educated in the belief, that sin brings many enjoyments in this world . . .

His position asks us to consider whether sin is truly fun. Does it really provide enjoyment? Does disrespect of self and others count as pleasure and value? Let us consider this in terms of "environmental sin." Living lightly on the Earth is sometimes portrayed as having to give up all that is fun and freeing, that somehow we are losing something by increasing fuel efficiency, recycling, and composting, and no longer using incandescent light bulbs. Do we truly lose anything by using a different light bulb? By recycling or composting? Are we somehow freer by disrespecting the Earth on which we live? Is this sin fun? Is it somehow enjoyable to avoid wind and solar technologies? Is environmental sin—ecological degradation—a pleasure?

Moreover, is it a pleasure to destroy the homelands and livelihoods of others through the effects of environmental sin? To poison food-bearing lands and waters through pollution, and then decide that these actions are harmless because the people they affect are African or Inuit or South Asian or poor or far away? No. It becomes impossible to see it that way when you look at the effects on the Earth and its peoples from the perspective of harming things and peoples that are precious and beloved, full of worth and dignity, and essentially good. We have the ability to learn and grow and change our cultural norms. Just as we have chosen to affirm the worth and dignity of all people, we have the ability to see the Earth not just as the place where our food grows, or mosquitoes and viruses live, but as something of value beyond our naming, something truly sacred.

In the poem "Fossil Fuel," John Dickson writes:

A scoop of coal revives the fireplace
and melts the chill that harbors in the bone
but soon releases ghosts of mastodons
and fish and flying reptiles
pressed in their carbon matrix since that day
when some upheaval trapped them in their bog.

What would happen if every time we used some petroleum, coal, or natural gas, we remembered that it was some prior life that created this ability to drive and heat and make electricity? Living things became this fuel that we use so thoughtlessly. Fear will not make us remember that life has become our fuel or that we should honor what has died every time we use oil and coal. A climate model's predictions will not remind us to love this world enough to save it.

We must recognize the inherent worth and dignity of each human and of all life—the inherent goodness of being and the interconnections that sustain and include us. Life on this planet is dynamic: There are times of decline and times of great fertility. The Earth is always perishing and the Earth is always being reborn, renewing itself. Our climate scientists are not crying wolf, but neither can they tell us the date, time, and exact coordinates of when the wolf will bite and how. Insisting that we know exactly what problems will occur in order to address the harm we inflict upon our Earth and one another misses the point. Our models predicting disaster are insufficient to inspire change. Our old theology of hell was insufficient, too, and so our theologians brought to bear their reason and insight to offer us another way into transformation.

Whether we are concerned with other people or the planet, we should limit our impact not because we're afraid, but because it's the right thing to do. Let us not make change because of some future hell, lest we link acting faithfully to fear, rather than love; lest we link action to disaster, rather than reverence. It is time for each of us to make one more choice that decreases the impact we have on the Earth, to use less, to enrich more. Let us make change because it is the right, respectful, loving thing to do now. Let us make more room for the other forms of existence that share the planet with us: human, plant, animal, mineral. Let us make change because sin—breaking relationship with that which we value and love—is not fun.

When it comes to the climate, each and every thing that we can do, from serving on a Unitarian Universalist environmental justice committee to turning off the water while brushing our teeth, makes a difference and is a necessary next act. Then we must reflect. Was this the best next act? Is there another next action to take? A better action? Will that next choice restore our relationships with other people, other communities and cultures, and with the Earth itself?

Through action and reflection grounded in cherishing our world, we can change our behavior and our national policy without anguish about not solving the entirety of the problem. We certainly hope to avoid the worst predictions that our scientists make. However, if we act out of our love for this Earth and all its inhabitants, we can avoid despair. In this, as in all things, our theology tells us to choose faith and hope and deep, abiding love over fear—to act from the knowledge that we will save what is of great worth and sacredness to us. Let us refuse to be made immobile by fear and despair, instead choosing one more faithful action in every moment. Let us remember our Universalist heritage and use that wisdom to chart a just, holy, and sustainable path forward.

TAKING IT FURTHER

Adam Robersmith emphasizes the value of making choices in the present moment due to the intrinsic value of those choices, irrespective of eventual outcomes. What choices are you making in your life today that support both environmental and racial justice? In the communities you belong to, what choices are these groups making that support environmental and racial justice?

. . . . .

Activism, of any kind, can lead to feelings of frustration or despair. How does your love for people and the environment ground your engagement?

. . . . .

Beyond what you are already doing today, what might be a next best action that you could take that would further deepen your commitment to environmental and racial justice?

PEGGY CLARKE AND MATTHEW McHALE

❖

Becoming Resilient:
Community Life for a New Age

A S OUR WORLD MOVES into an uncertain future, beset by social, ecological, and economic crises, the fact that we seem unable to pull ourselves off the path of destruction has many of us terrified and confounded. Even those who can clearly see the cliff we are barreling toward have a hard time envisioning, much less articulating, an alternative to the dominant political-economic system that has its foot on the accelerator. As Fredric Jameson quips in *New Left Review*, it's "easier for us to imagine the end of the world than the end of capitalism." Thus one of the most vital tasks in these times is to imagine alternatives to continuing business as usual; alternatives that offer us a way off the path of ecological destruction, and also reject the unjust and oppressive realities of the dominant system, in favor of a resilient and life-sustaining society.

As a religious people we can think of this as living into the prophetic tradition. In *The Prophetic Imagination*, theologian Walter Brueggemann writes that while we often think of prophetic ministry as simply decrying the injustices of society, it's more broadly about nurturing, nourishing, and evoking "a consciousness and perception alternative to consciousness and perception of the dominant culture around us." Every prophetic act "is part of a way of evoking, forming, and reforming an alternative community." With their unique position in our society, religious communities can play a vital role in experimenting with and modeling alternative ways of living.

At this critical juncture, our world needs our congregations to be models of the life-sustaining society we want to create. While some congregations are taking important steps in that direction, they remain small in number and none are living up to their true potential. In this essay we explore some of the dynamics holding congregations back, and how the model of "resilience-based organizing" can help our congregations live into that vision in powerful and transformative ways.

RESILIENCE-BASED ORGANIZING

Around the time Hurricane Katrina hit in 2005, a group of San Francisco Bay Area organizers of color wanted to explore the opportunities and challenges facing working class communities of color in relationship to ecology and sustainability. They took an intersectional approach, which organizer Gopal Dayaneni says recognizes "the relationship between social inequity—like racial, gender, and economic injustice—and ecological erosion." Those organizers coalesced into Movement Generation, a movement-building organization offering trainings, resources, and support to social movements led by low-income communities and communities of color.

They identified four "R"s as necessary aspects of transformative justice work: Resistance—fighting against the destructive aspects of the dominant system; Resilience—building our capacity to survive, thrive, and navigate change; Restoring living systems and ecological integrity; and Reimagining a different world. Rather than traditional campaign-based organizing that focuses on resistance—organizing around an identified problem or issue and trying to get laws or regulations passed to address it—Movement Generation developed a resilience-based organizing model.

"The best acts of resistance are acts of resilience," says Dayaneni, one of Movement Generation's core organizers. "When we actually create the solutions that create resilience and capacity to navigate change well as a community, that in and of itself can be an act of resistance."

According to an article on the Movement Generation website, resilience-based organizing is grounded in the idea that "transformative social change requires that we organize communities into a collective effort to meet the need at hand through direct democratic decision-making and physical implementation by those who are being impacted by the problem." Its organizing approach is rooted in community "in a way that reorients power to be more local and democratic; rather than simply trying to win concessions from corporations, or the structures of government that serve them." This approach finds inspiration from groups like the Black Panther

Party and Brazil's Landless Workers Movement (Movimento dos Trabalhadores Rurais Sem Terra, or the MST).

While most commonly remembered for "policing the police" in Black communities and the sometimes deadly conflicts with the police and FBI that resulted, the Black Panthers also devoted tremendous energy to "survival programs." Through these programs, say Joshua Bloom and Waldo E. Martin Jr. in *Black against Empire: The History and Politics of the Black Panther Party*, the Panthers provided free services to communities otherwise denied access to rights and resources: the wildly successful Free Breakfast for School Children program, which fed tens of thousands of children nationwide; free medical clinics; drug and alcohol rehabilitation programs; classes on politics and economics; clothing distribution; and more.

The MST is a movement in Brazil composed of hundreds of thousands of rural workers fighting for land reform in a country where 1.6 percent of the landowners control almost half of the land suitable for growing food. Since 1984, the MST has peacefully occupied unused land, securing 18.5 million acres for about 370,000 families across 2,000 settlements. According to its website, the MST's organizing approach has been one of creating community resilience through establishing food security through the cooperative farms they set up; constructing houses, schools, and clinics to meet the local groups' needs while they work toward environmental sustainability; and promoting Indigenous culture and gender equality.

"Instead of making demands on existing power holders to do what we want them to do, we're going to do what needs to happen, in a way that articulates its righteousness as action and its beauty as vision," says Movement Generation's Dayaneni. "We want to take action as the expression of our organizing. The actions themselves don't create the [systemic] transformation we need; it's the organizing that does." The Black Panthers' survival programs made their communities more resilient, deepening and expanding their political power, which also made them a greater threat to the racist status quo. In a memo to special agents, FBI Director J. Edgar Hoover called the Free Breakfast for School Children program the "greatest threat" the Black Panther Party posed. Through the MST's organizing, and the resilience underlying it, they have grown from a few thousand people into a formidable force in Brazil that offers "a concrete alternative to today's globalization that puts profits before people and humanity."

CONGREGATIONS AS CENTERS FOR COMMUNITY RESILIENCE

Our religious communities have the potential to become models of the future we want to create. Yet the twentieth-century prototype of congregational life is insufficient for the radical changes we face in the twenty-first century. As much as we may love our Sunday worship, faith development classes, potlucks, and even committee meetings, these alone will not carry us into the new age.

Life as we know it is dramatically changing. With global temperatures rising at alarming rates, we are already seeing the effects of drought on food systems, rising sea levels on island nations and coastal towns, increased intensity of storms on our cities, and melting ice caps on access to fresh water. Mitigating this frightening trend will require a World War II– scale effort. While such an effort needs governmental support, the real shift will happen in small pockets throughout the world. Unlike WWII, we aren't transforming an economic system temporarily; we are transforming all of our systems permanently. To do that successfully, houses of worship will need to become centers of hope and resilience.

Resilient congregations will be fully engaged in their communities. They will provide a meeting place for community organizing and shelter after natural disasters. They will be learning centers for the necessary process of "reskilling"— growing food, repairing things, building naturally, maintaining renewable energy systems. They might even provide land on which we can grow our food together. We can imagine congregations hosting free-sharing sites, and ways for people to barter services, allowing us to shift away from an economic system that relies on endless growth.

This is a vision some congregations already have for themselves, but very few truly live up to the exciting and necessary potential. We see three distinct reasons for this: Congregations focus a lot of energy and attention on themselves, losing sight of the world around them; congregational justice work is supported theoretically and sometimes financially by a large group, but the work is done by a tiny percentage of its members; and congregations lack the necessary skills for authentic partnership, especially with marginalized communities.

Given these limitations, once we have the vision, where might we begin? We suggest taking time, perhaps at a congregational meeting, to help everyone understand the vision and their role in bringing it into reality. Living out this vision might require letting go of other things, some beloved and some that we habitually spend a tremendous amount of energy on.

Any acts of resistance should also build community and power. If it's always the same small group, you can only accomplish small things. So when planning an action or activity, consider how to involve more people, which will probably require multiple paths for engagement.

For example, co-author of this essay Matthew McHale helped start a food forest during his internship at West Shore UU Church, near Cleveland. A food forest—or forest garden—is designed to mimic a dense woodland ecosystem, which, by honoring ecological interdependence, is largely self-sustaining. In early spring, we kicked off with a multi-generational seed-planting party. Several people took the seeds home, where they sprouted into seedlings that were sold at a plant sale and swap, raising funds and building momentum for the project. Next, we "lasagna-mulched" the land in preparation for the food forest. Most people got to work with shovels and rakes, while others collected compost, wood chips, and cardboard for the mulch. Some contributed in less physically demanding ways, like recruiting volunteers and preparing food for the work party. While the mulch decomposed, community leaders taught a course on permaculture, the sustainable agricultural model underlying a food forest. The course culminated with participants collectively developing the landscape design for the food forest. Over a few months, a handful of individuals grew into several dozen who were involved in creating it—before a single plant was even in the ground. Three years later the food forest is thriving and has been expanded to more of the church campus.

Yet, for all its success, this project was still inwardly focused. In order to really live into resilience-based organizing, it's vital to engage the wider community. A food forest planted in one of Cleveland's numerous vacant lots has a different impact than one on church grounds. A direct action done in partnership with a community organization has more power than one organized in isolation.

How can we ensure that our work is vital and serves the wider community? We can start by identifying local "frontline communities"—low-income communities and communities of color who bear the brunt of the devastation of the modern industrial system and who are leaders in the struggle to shift toward a more just and sustainable future. Often lacking access to land, clean water and air, healthy and affordable food, and healthcare, frontline communities are among the most vulnerable. But we can't simply swoop in and try to paternalistically fix their problems—it would have been misguided to plant a food forest in a food desert without working with the local residents. People organizing on the frontlines know what their communities need and have the knowledge and skills to help meet those needs. We need to be working in solidarity, which means joining them in their struggles. Rather than trying to come in as a savior, solidarity requires listening, relationship-building, humility, and a willingness to take on a support role when asked.

As we move deeper into this age of climate disruption, ecological erosion, and social upheaval, resilient communities are necessary for our collective survival. Our capacity to navigate change will determine the level of our success as we enter a new reality. Solidarity with frontline communities—with a clear understanding of a need for intersectional responses that address racial, gender, and economic inequality—is critical. Without authentic partnership and without clearly understanding the systemic transformation required, our response to the current climate crisis will be insufficient. We are facing an almost incomprehensible emergency, and until now we haven't had the skills or vision to adequately address it. Building resilient communities is the transformative response these times demand.

TAKING IT FURTHER

Peggy Clarke and Matthew McHale invite us to think about frontline communities, often communities of color that are directly impacted by issues of environment and race. What are those communities in your local region and what issues are they working on? How might you and your community develop or deepen relationship in solidarity with those who are in frontline communities?

· · · · ·

Collaboration with frontline communities requires that we engage in the ongoing work of building and deepening our lens of racial and societal analysis. Read *Waking Up White, and Finding Myself in the Story of Race* (2014) by Debby Irving as a way to begin or continue such reflection.

· · · · ·

Consider engaging in Movement Generation's "Find Your Frontlines" activity, or one of their other activities, available here: www.movementgeneration.org/resources/curriculum-tools.

KATHLEEN McTIGUE

❖

Drawing on the Deep Waters: Contemplative Practice in Justice-Making

W HAT DOES IT MEAN to be a practicing Unitarian Universalist?

Ask this question of a dozen Unitarian Universalists, and you will get more than a dozen answers! But you can be pretty certain that most of those answers will have something to do with taking action on behalf of justice. We have little consensus in the realm of theology and beliefs, but we agree broadly that any religion worth the name should help shift our behaviors and actions toward the greater good. So we articulate the meaning and practice of our faith not with creedal statements or expectations of spiritual practice—since even church attendance is optional—but through the actions that reveal and enact our core values.

In a world flawed and twisted by deep fissures of inequality and oppression, this social justice dimension of our faith is necessary and laudable, but insufficient. What is too often missing is the acknowledgment that our lives are shaped by

inner as well as outer work—and that the outer work of justice can be made more powerful and effective when joined to
the inner work accomplished through spiritual disciplines.

Spiritual practices come in widely varied forms, drawn
from many centuries of human invention across every culture.
They include collective worship; collective or solitary prayer
or meditation; movement practices like yoga, tai chi, or dance;
and disciplines of chant, song, and writing. Done with care and
intention, we can turn many routine elements of our lives into
a practice: a walk down our street or in the woods, playing the
piano, even riding a crowded subway in the thick of rush hour.

Despite their many variations, three essential threads weave
through all spiritual practices: intention, attention, and repetition. Intention is the deliberate engagement of our will, in
a practice that nurtures a sense of connection to something
bigger than ourselves. Attention means we exist only in the
present moment: We practice quieting the incessant chatter of
our minds in order to receive one moment at a time with
openness, curiosity, and a willingness to be with what is. Repetition allows our centering activity to form part of the rhythm
of our day, and in the same way that constant practice allows
us to become a musician or learn a new language, repetition
of a spiritual practice helps us hone qualities like awareness,
patience, and compassion.

The long labors of social justice can certainly be undertaken by people with purely secular convictions, driven by
political and ethical concerns. Yet if we also want our activism
to reflect our faith, there are compelling reasons to dedicate

ourselves to a spiritual practice—especially when we turn to the extraordinary challenges of climate change. I have identified five of those reasons, though many others could be found.

Spiritual practices ground us in something bigger than ourselves. Jewish theologian Abraham Joshua Heschel wrote, "Living is not a private affair of the individual. Living is what we do with God's time, what we do with God's world." We need not believe in God in order to grasp Heschel's meaning. We live in a society in which we are often encouraged to regard our living very much as an individual affair, and that delusion is toxic to the health, well-being, and even survival of our fragile planet.

We are part of an immense, living reality, and the choices we make make an impact on that reality far beyond our small field of awareness. Understanding that truth on a spiritual level allows us to make choices in our daily lives and our justice work that align our individual actions with the well-being of the whole. We need to cultivate the capacity to bow to that which is so much larger than ourselves, to acknowledge the vast mystery of our universe, and to feel ourselves a part of that immensity. There is an essential humility in this: However confused we might be about the notion of God, we are reminded that we ourselves alone are not God. We are connected to and are part of a vast unfolding that we cannot entirely grasp. We do not have all the answers, and we do well to remember it. When we approach our justice work with this kind of humility, we become more open to the ideas of others, more capable of being flexible and adaptive, and less egocentric. Knowing on a deep and intrinsic level of our being that we are only part of the whole allows us to collaborate more effectively and to add our unique gifts as one part of the whole, which is greater than all its individuals.

Spiritual practices help us stay in the present moment. We spend an enormous amount of time, attention, and energy on the incessant stories that play out in our own heads, often quite unconsciously. If you've never noticed this, it can be quite revealing to simply listen to your own inner monologue for a few minutes as you walk down a street or sit staring out the window. The mind drifts or flits from one topic to the next with no connection or transition: "What in the world is she thinking, wearing a top like that? I wonder if it's going to rain today—can't quite see the horizon, looks like some clouds are . . . Whoa, what was that sound? Oh, shoot, I have to remember to buy my plane ticket for next month, and what time is that meeting this afternoon again, before or after lunch? Wow, that dude is tall. I can't believe what Joe said to me, totally out of the blue. I'm going for that pizza again today, but maybe I should just have salad, I hate the way my stomach pooches out. Will that blue dress still fit? I wonder whether those earthquakes in Nepal are really over, poor people. Maybe I should climb the Himalayas someday, something else for the bucket list. Why is that jerk talking so loudly, he shouldn't even be using his cell phone here. . . ."

If you really focus in on it, the nature of this running commentary is appalling: It is repetitive, boring, and judgmental.

But that little busybody in our heads—what Buddhism calls our "monkey mind"—does more than issue banal commentary. It tells us stories about our reality, moment to moment, and those stories take up so much space that they can block the view: We see what our minds are telling us to see, rather than what's really there. We are particularly vulnerable to this when our emotions are involved. When the story is something that makes us angry or anxious, or when it makes us eager and greedy, we can trick ourselves into reacting to our own expectations or projections.

Spiritual practices help quiet the noise in our own heads. This in turn allows a little more room for us to focus and absorb what is actually going on, and separate that reality from the stories. We can hold ourselves open to learning directly from the person or situation in front of us. We can choose more deliberately whether and how to respond.

In justice work, this translates into taking actions that are strategic, rather than reactive. When we quiet our habitual minds and the emotions around the justice issue, we are more capable of understanding the truth and of creating an effective plan to change injustice to justice. Being present to the reality of the moment instead of our stories of fear, desire, and illusion also helps us maintain better relationships in our organizing communities. Like all human communities, those organizing for justice often struggle with internal conflict that arises from members triggering unexamined emotional reactions in one another. A spiritual practice of quieting the mind and developing self-awareness reduces this type of conflict and makes our communities more effective in their justice work.

Spiritual practices cultivate the qualities we most want to bring forward. Human beings are creatures of aspiration. Most of us are aware of at least some of our shortcomings—our hair-trigger temper, our impatience, our selfishness. We also know what it's like to overcome these tendencies and bring forth our best selves: to deliberately calm our burst of temper, or consciously relax our impatience, or extend ourselves into generosity. Across cultures and languages there are a handful of virtues that people everywhere hope to cultivate and manifest in themselves: generosity, compassion, forgiveness, courage, steadfastness, kindness.

Some lucky souls may have these qualities as their default settings, but for the rest of us they require deliberate effort.

One day in mid-November I got on a train from New York to Boston, which is a lovely half-day trip. The train rolls along the coast through a variety of urban, neighborhood, and suburban communities, and interspersed there are long stretches of woods and water: bayside, seaside, tidal marsh, and ponds. On this particular day the clouds were thick and low and a steady rain had just started to fall as we trundled along. In a seat behind me, a young man finished up a phone conversation by saying, "Yeah, it's turned into a disgusting day, dark and rainy. Lots of fog. It's supposed to get even colder tomorrow. I hate New England." Just a few minutes later, a cell phone rang a couple of seats ahead of me. I heard a man's voice answer, and then say in a note of bright cheeriness, "Oh,

I'm great! It's a beautiful day, rainy and cool with this soft fog drifting through the trees, so peaceful. What a treat!"

There are lots of different channels we can dial into for our perspective on the world. Sometimes almost without even noticing, we dial into the channels of complaint or crabbiness, of distraction or impatience. Despite what we aim for in our moments of high aspiration, we get caught up in the small stuff. Spiritual practices help tilt us back toward our aspirations. They remind us that the virtues we admire in others are actually states of mind and ways of action that we can choose. The more we practice them, the more widely we open ourselves to a different perception and a changed story, to becoming the person who looks at the rain and says, "What a treat!"

In our work for justice, our best selves bring out the best in each other and in our communities. We develop deeper, healthier relationships with one another, and these connections carry us through the struggles of facing the world's injustice. We create communities of care and resilience that support our work in the world. When we bring a perspective of gratitude and appreciation, the community and the work become more enjoyable. Rather than being something we do out of obligation, it becomes something we do because we like it. More people show up more often. We are nourished by the work instead of drained by it.

Spiritual practices remind us that the things we want to change in the world also exist in ourselves. The fifteenth-century Sufi poet Kabir, as translated by Robert Bly, wrote:

I don't know what sort of a God we have been
    talking about.
The caller calls in a loud voice to the Holy One
    at dusk.
Why? Surely the Holy One is not deaf.
He hears the delicate anklets that ring on the
    feet of an insect as it walks.
Go over and over your beads, paint weird
    designs on your forehead,
wear your hair matted, long, and ostentatious,
but when deep inside you there is a loaded gun,
    how can you have God?

If deep inside us there is a loaded gun, how can we have
God? If deep inside us we are seething with anger, how shall
we be peacemakers? If deep inside us there are the seeds of
greed, how will we shift the grotesque chasm between the
rich and the poor? Spiritual practices keep us honest, mindful of the fact that the changes we want to work for in our
world need to be undertaken with a willingness to be changed
ourselves.

Spiritual practices help sustain us through confusion and despair.
Social change is long, hard work, and it often seems to be
punctuated by setbacks and defeats more often than by victories. When we set out to put the small influence of our lives
into the struggle for justice, we cannot expect that the vision
we hold for a better world will be realized soon or easily, or
even in the course of our lifetimes. This is even more true as

we engage the many intersecting issues of climate change. We will face challenges that are unpredictable, multifaceted, and enormous.

In the face of these challenges, it is essential that we draw on the deep waters of spiritual practices that renew and sustain our spirits. These practices do not resolve the problems we face, nor do they magically take away the feelings that arise when we see the true dimensions of these problems. Despair, discouragement, helplessness, and confusion may all still go parading through our hearts—but spiritual practices help us hold them within a larger context.

Buddhism teaches about this with the analogy of a glass of very salty water. Imagine our suffering and despair as that glass of salt water: drinking it is unbearable, impossible. But if we take those feelings and reactions into our spiritual practice, it's like carrying that glass of salty water to the edges of a clear lake and pouring it in. The salt is all still there, but now it's part of a larger reality.

Spiritual practices help us reach those sustaining waters. There we remember all who taught compassion, all who have acted for justice, and we recall that in the long arc toward justice, our best efforts are just one small part. This allows us to hold even our despair within the larger frame of this lifetime work. Grounded again in hope, we can then bring that hope back out with us, to all the others who are struggling to find their way in this beautiful, fragile, difficult world.

TAKING IT FURTHER

Kathleen McTigue invites us to ground our justice work in contemplative and other spiritual practices as a way of staying grounded and as a way of mediating any feelings that may arise with this work. What current spiritual practices, if any, are you engaged in? Have you been a part of justice-building work that has integrated spiritual practices? If so, what were they?

. . . . .

Consider experimenting with spiritual practices, such as Buddhist tonglen meditation. Joan Halifax provides helpful instructions and guidance that are available here: www.upaya.org/dox/Tonglen.pdf. How might such a practice allow one to connect with the suffering of marginalized communities?

. . . . .

Contemplative and spiritual practices span a wide range of possibilities, and often we need to find the ones that personally connect with and work for each of us. Read *Everyday Spiritual Practice: Simple Pathways for Enriching Your Life* (1999) edited by Scott W. Alexander, as a way of exploring what practices might speak to you.

PAMELA SPARR

❖

Transforming Unitarian Universalist Culture: Stepping Out of Our Silos and Selves

I N THE SUMMER OF 2016 I had the privilege of teaching at the Eliot Institute in Washington State for a week. My theme was "Creating a Climate of Justice," which looked at climate change through an anti-racism/anti-oppression lens. A few months before the camp, the deans warned me that some campers were worried about how depressing the morning presentations might be and were saying they didn't want to spend their summer vacation being "bummed out." My challenge was to talk about one of the most pressing moral issues of our day in a way that inspired and moved the adults to action rather than reinforce whatever paralysis and despair they might be experiencing. How was I going to keep an audience past Day One when everyone could easily vote with their feet and go outdoors to enjoy the gorgeous Pacific Northwest surroundings?

Many of us have sat through mind- and soul-numbing presentations about greenhouse gas levels, predictions for sea-level rise, debates about whether the Earth has reached a tipping point, and what kind of CO_2 reduction levels need to be set. So we may understand the campers' concerns. Or, we may have taken this scientific approach ourselves as we tried to galvanize interest and action. Scientists the world over have played an invaluable role in addressing the climate crisis. They have spoken the truth when not everyone has wanted to hear it, raised crucial red flags of alarm, and offered important insights about productive technical solutions. However, as we have discovered, when it comes to climate change, the truth hasn't set us free.

It hasn't set us free as Unitarian Universalists because our approach often has been emotionally and spiritually sterile. It has often failed to be sufficiently rigorous in understanding and integrating racial, economic, and gender justice dimensions at its core. And it hasn't been sufficiently inspiring, bold, inclusive, and collaborative in crafting a vision of the way forward.

Cornel West, Joanna Macy, and many others have addressed how we as individuals can live with integrity and "active hope" at this particular moment. And there are many inspiring and instructive examples of current organizing to guide us. I'd like to explore how this confluence of challenges and opportunities calls us collectively as Unitarian Universalists to transform our congregations and institutions, and how we show up in the much-needed communal work of building the Beloved Community. I offer these perspectives from my personal life of activism in and outside my home congregation, and my professional life working on justice issues for a variety of secular and religious organizations, including three Unitarian Universalist ones. These views are strictly my own. I hope that they contribute to the exciting conversations and projects that have already begun.

If we are to be all that we can be collectively at this moment, and joyfully and effectively contribute to what some authors call "the Great Turning," we must transform our denominational culture in at least five ways:

- offer a bolder prophetic imagination
- develop the courage and capacity to talk religiously
- get out of our silos and off the farm
- engage in radical relationship building
- become more countercultural

PROPHETIC IMAGINATION

In *This Changes Everything: Capitalism vs. the Climate*, Naomi Klein makes a compelling argument about the need for economic, political, and social revolutions if we are to curb climate change in time. Unfortunately, she ignores the role of religion and religious bodies in her analysis. Yet, when she lays out an agenda for change, some of the key pieces are squarely the responsibility of faith communities. She writes,

> Fundamentally, the task is to articulate not just an alternative set of policy proposals but an alternative worldview to rival the one at the heart of the ecological crisis—embedded in interdependence rather than

hyper-individualism, reciprocity rather than dominance, and cooperation rather than hierarchy. . . . This
is another lesson from the transformative movements
of the past: all of them understood that the process of
shifting cultural values . . . was central to their work.
And so they dreamed in public, showed humanity a
better version of itself, modeled different values in their
own behavior, and in the process liberated the political imagination and rapidly altered the sense of what
was possible. They were also unafraid of the language
of morality—to give the pragmatic, cost/benefit argu-
ments a rest and speak of right and wrong, of love and
indignation.

Providing a moral analysis; offering a powerful, inspiring,
values-based, justice-oriented worldview; and being the
change we wish to see in the world are all the work of a faith
community. The worldwide anticipation of Pope Francis's
environmental encyclical was palpable—within and well
beyond the Catholic community—as was the joy when it
was issued. That reaction is a testament to a need, a craving for
progressive religious leaders to frame major issues of our day
in moral and spiritual terms. The reaction also is an example
of a collective wish for our religious leaders to be bolder and
more public in naming the powers and principalities, the
structural forms of injustice at work in the world, and to call
us to our higher selves in creating a different reality—to provide a prophetic imagination. My sense is that many Unitarian Universalists are hungry for more of that from the pulpit

as well as from our denominational leaders. Many in our communities who may or may not have a religious affiliation are too. Offering this kind of consistent vision and voice is not just the responsibility of our clergy; it is also the task of our collective community.

Many of our congregations have led the way in their communities by purchasing renewable energy, replacing lightbulbs, weatherizing buildings, and installing solar panels. These are important steps to demonstrate how to reduce carbon emissions, but while they are necessary, generally they are insufficient for exemplifying prophetic moral imagination. This is because they do not require us to change our relationships of privilege and power to other people. They do not require us to change our economic or political system. They hint at but do not directly speak the language of morality.

William Barber II's "Moral Mondays" in North Carolina address this craving for a bolder public witness, for a prophetic imagination that captivates and galvanizes us to build Beloved Community. At the Eliot Institute, when we looked at some of the components of a transformed world, and our transformed being that would contribute to climate justice, we examined how we could live as individuals, families, and as a community from a sense of awe, wonder, gratitude, radical hospitality, solidarity, mutual liberation, and hope. We wondered how we might live into these qualities in a way that is prophetic. One very practical example that captivated many campers was to explore how to live into radical hospitality. Some municipalities in the US and other countries allow residents who are not citizens to vote in local elections. In fact, a hundred years ago, more than twenty US states allowed this, until we entered another period of anti-immigrant distrust and bias. As wars, civil unrest, economic desperation, and climate change force more people to flee their home countries, we can take our love and "comprehensive immigration reform" to a whole new level.

COURAGE AND CAPACITY
TO TALK RELIGIOUSLY

If we are to exercise prophetic imagination, we need to be comfortable and fluent in "talking religiously." In *Reclaiming Public Witness: Liberal Religion in the Public Square*, Unitarian Universalist theologian Paul Rasor cogently assesses our discomfort, the fallacies and tensions behind our unwillingness to adopt this vocabulary, and what it means to speak religiously.

Rasor claims that at times liberal religious identity is so "thin" that it basically evaporates and gets expressed as simply a liberal political position. This happens in some of our environmental and climate work—although that is beginning to change. We're living a kind of odd paradox. Colleagues inside and outside our denomination have said that Unitarian Universalists have the reputation of being "the people who show up." One inspiring example of this was our attendance at the People's Climate March in New York City in the fall of 2014. Reportedly, there were at least fifteen hundred Unitarian Universalists on the streets, which, if accurate, means that we were one of the largest, if not the largest, organized faith delegations there. Similarly, Unitarian Universalists often are overrepresented among the membership and leadership of many environmental and climate change organizations compared to our numbers in the population. Yet, when Unitarian Universalists are involved in those groups, leaders report that they often are religiously invisible and inarticulate, even in ecumenical and interfaith circles, where talking religiously is encouraged.

The customary stance for many Unitarian Universalists is to work on climate and environmental justice issues in a way that sounds like we are from the Sierra Club or Audubon Society—or, perhaps for younger activists, the Our Power Campaign or Movement Generation—even when we are educating and organizing within our congregations. Our challenge is to move out of our secular skin and to wear our Unitarian Universalist skin all the time. This means framing concerns and proposed solutions in moral terms inside and outside of our congregational walls. It means speaking and organizing from a place of hope rather than fear. It means making the pursuit of justice—not technical solutions— central to our vision and strategy. It also means we need to organize and analyze situations differently than our secular counterparts.

For example, faith-based and faith-rooted organizing use different understandings of how to gather and use power and how to relate to any opposition. Faith-based and faith-rooted organizers approach power differently, preferring to use "power with" (horizontal collaboration) rather than hierarchical "power over" and growing "power to" (personal agency). This approach to organizing also understands and practices solidarity differently. Traditionally, labor and other kinds of political and social groups practice solidarity by saying, "I'll stop what I am doing and come support you, if you do the same when I need that." Faith-rooted solidarity is not transactional. It might be described as *universal relational* because its adherents say, "I know that my well-being is totally and irrevocably tied up with yours. My liberation is dependent on yours." It's not a quid-pro-quo give and take. Rather, it says, "I am there for you always." Another key difference is how one understands, sees, and refers to the opposition. Faith-based and faith-rooted organizers generally do not "other" their opposition by labeling them as enemies. We recognize that we may share some of the values, attitudes, and behaviors of our opposition—positive qualities that unite us in our humanity, as well as unhelpful qualities that mean we also are a part of the problem—and in working for Beloved Community, realize our own liberation is tied up with everyone else's.

There are three reasons why this is important. First, as Naomi Klein points out, there is vital work to be done in shifting values, lifting up a compelling, alternative moral vision, and being an example of the change we wish to see. We can more fully and authentically do this when we claim our identity and authority as religious persons. Secondly, as Paul Rasor notes, by not claiming our religious identity and speaking from that place within ourselves, we undermine our convictions and leave a vacuum, a gap, in the public square. In the current political and cultural context, that gap tends to get filled with hate speech, negativity, and narrow visions. We cede territory unnecessarily. Finally, it is a matter of integrity. We embrace Unitarian Universalism not just on Sunday mornings or whenever we meet in community; our faith is 24/7. Leading national pollsters consistently have encouraged the religious community to talk about their faith and values when lobbying their elected representatives about climate change, saying that politicians invite this as a way of stepping aside from otherwise deep partisan divides.

Given the immense damage Indigenous peoples, racial and ethnic minorities, women, and those living in poverty around the world (and in our own country) experience as a result of climate change, fossil fuel extraction, and the pollution generated from fossil fuel–burning facilities, it is imperative that we are comfortable and articulate when framing our concerns and solutions out of our profound sense of the sacredness of all life, of our respect for the dignity and worth of every individual, of every threatened species. We can express our wonder and awe, our love of the mystery and complexity of the web of life, and our deep desire to protect the integrity of the natural world. We can talk about how the integrity of our soul and spirit is bound up with the well-being of others—other humans and the more-than-human world.

While seminary training prepares Unitarian Universalist clergy to speak religiously, laypeople often are left to their own devices. We come from a wide range of backgrounds, and may or may not take religious education classes that can help us understand our unique theological and spiritual grounding on any particular issue. This puts us at a disadvantage when working with other religious folk who come from traditions that offer, or even require, a deeper form of lay theological education. It raises the question of whether we need to rethink some of the religious education we offer youth and adults to better prepare them for the kind of religious discourse and activism this time calls for. It also raises the question about the need to offer basic theological education in the preparation and training of lay social justice leaders. And finally, it highlights whether we have sufficient uniquely Unitarian Universalist ecological and climate justice–oriented theological and spiritual materials for religious educators and other leaders willing to train us. This final question may apply to other justice arenas as well.

GET OUT OF OUR SILOS AND OFF THE FARM

We face so many soul-damaging and life-threatening challenges at this historical moment: an unprecedented global climate crisis; tremendous economic inequalities; a highly militarized, violence-prone, and brutalizing culture of death and disposability; deep racial/ethnic divisions, discrimination, fear, and mistrust; and a corporate stranglehold on our political system, which makes a mockery of democracy and stymies needed change.

We often operate in narrow silos of particular interests—both within our congregations and in national organizations. Those who work on environmental or climate issues don't talk with those interested in racial justice or who work on affordable housing or mass incarceration. The group interested in inequality issues is in its own corner. And the people who care about multiple issues get burned out going to so many meetings. This siloed situation has to change if we are to preserve our sanity and health and maximize our effectiveness.

Justice issues are inherently interconnected, especially climate justice. As Naomi Klein points out, climate change does not need a new movement, but rather a coming together of all extant liberation movements. Climate change offers us the opportunity to complete critical unfinished business on many fronts at once. We can see these intertwined threads in the way Big Oil dominates our political system. We see these threads in the placement of coal-fired power plants in communities of color, which bear the negative health consequences. We see these threads in the impact of climate change on the education of girls and their marrying age in some nations of the Global South. We see the legacy of colonialism and imperialism in the role the US has played in climate negotiations. These are just a few of the dense tapestries of connections between various issues and their underlying structural roots.

When we pay attention to synergies between issues when crafting or participating in projects to address injustice, it can create positive change in multiple arenas simultaneously. It may be easier for us to engage in a multidimensional initiative if we "get off the farm" (i.e., go outside our congregation or particular organization) to join with others. Great synergistic partners and projects may be right outside our door, right around the corner, or in the next town over. This may require us to reorient our gaze in a different direction, to develop relationships inside and outside our congregation or institution with people and groups we don't yet know, to loosen our grip on tightly held agendas. The results can be truly amazing.

One inspiring example of a synergistic solution to multiple problems is the Evergreen Cooperatives in Cleveland. For some years, the Democracy Collaborative has been interested in building wealth in low-income communities of color in the US. Their strategy is to build "green" cooperative businesses using local anchor institutions such as universities and hospitals to serve as an initial customer base for the co-ops. Their first venture was in Hough, an especially challenged neighborhood in an especially challenged city. Cleveland is second only to Detroit in levels of poverty, chronic unemployment and underemployment, population loss, abandoned homes, and tax base erosion. Hough is a predominantly African-American neighborhood that burned after Martin Luther King Jr. was assassinated, and never recovered. Presently, three co-ops (handling laundry, producing solar electricity, and growing hydroponic vegetables) are up and running, with two more on the drawing board. The plan is to enable worker-owners to have about $60,000 in equity within about five years. Additionally, the co-ops have worked out a deal with county officials for interested worker-owners to buy houses and have their mortgage payments deducted from their paychecks, further stabilizing neighborhoods and the workers' lives. Many of the workers have spent time in prison, and the co-op jobs represent a vital second chance. The greenhouse donates 10 percent of its harvest to local families, helping to improve the nutrition and health of local residents. Until the greenhouses started growing it, lettuce sold in Cleveland generally came from two thousand miles away. So, all three co-ops in their own ways reduce carbon emissions, promote sustainable and just economic development, address systemic racism and inequality, promote restorative justice, and improve health outcomes in the neighborhood. The Democracy Collaborative is now spreading this model to other cities.

As congregations and individuals shift investments and endowments away from fossil fuels to more community-enhancing ventures, they can advocate for and finance synergistic enterprises to better leverage their resources.

RADICAL RELATIONSHIP BUILDING

In order to "get off the farm," many of us need to learn new relational and partnership skills. National denominational staff and other Unitarian Universalist leaders are helping congregations become more multicultural and more capable of boundary-crossing partnerships. This is exceedingly important work. We have a successful brand—Standing on the Side of Love—which manifests in a heartening sea of yellow shirts and liturgical stoles at marches and vigils across the nation. We have some inspiring congregational examples of boundary-crossing solidarity, such as those deeply involved in immigration advocacy. We have an energetic group of Unitarian Universalists eager to spearhead class conversations. We have an incredible reputation for our LGBTQ work. Yet, we still have a long way to go to get outside our walls and comfort zones to cultivate the breadth and depth of relationships these times demand.

One of the dimensions of diversity and radical relationship building that does not seem to get as much of our attention is theological diversity. For example, a significant number of the state executive directors for Interfaith Power and Light are Unitarian Universalists, at least in part because of our comfort with theological diversity. But how far does this comfort extend? Is it contingent on not too much overtly religious talk, a focus on a political or practical task at hand, or some assumed underlying shared political or class identity?

I raise this question because in my years of climate advocacy, I've noticed an interesting trend. One of the traditions that has been most willing to use its full muscle to advocate for policy change and accountability, most willing to put its bodies on the line and get arrested, is the Christian evangelical movement. Progressive evangelicals like Jim Wallace and the Sojourners community were the first to make a commitment to climate justice. Since then, more theologically conservative evangelicals also have been addressing environmental and climate justice in some very interesting ways. If we have any hope of successfully tackling the power of the Koch Brothers, of addressing climate change, of building the Beloved Community, we are going to have to stretch ourselves to befriend and collaborate with many different types of people and movements, including those with whom some of us may feel theologically uncomfortable.

PAMELA SPARR

GOING COUNTERCULTURAL

These times demand more than a radical, prophetic vision and voice. We also are called to create communities of resilience related to the effects of climate change and of resistance to the cultural, economic, and political status quo. Theologians like Thomas Berry, psychologists like Bill Plotkin, journalists like Naomi Klein, and many others argue that we are addicted to Western civilization, and that part of the Great Turning involves renouncing this addiction. A major project of any religious tradition involves providing needed spiritual nurture and resources for all of us to get into recovery, and institutional spaces to foster individual and collective resistance.

If we are serious about fostering recovery and resistance, we will need a robust denomination-wide conversation about what this really means. Rethinking how we live in order to better reflect our values and vision—as well as to interrupt the dynamics of division and destruction—takes time, energy, input from others, and support. This deep work will challenge many of our comforts, assumptions, and habits, and it won't be easy or popular. How can our congregations and national organizations create the kind of spaces, conversations, and resources to help us all do this? How can we as individuals and as congregations support our clergy and national organizations to show this kind of leadership, particularly in a context of concern over declining membership and sketchy finances?

Encouraging resistance to the status quo offers us an opportunity to reclaim some of our historical heritage by creating and investing in alternative models of church and living arrangements. Some contemporary Christian and Jewish groups have created alternative communities in various US cities as a way of living out more countercultural values. Why can't we? Some young adult Unitarian Universalists are experimenting with collective housing arrangements that blend practical needs with political and spiritual aspirations, while others are forming deep covenantal groups in their communities. These communities illustrate various aspects of what living in a climate-just way can mean: simplicity, less focus on materialism and individualism, integrating spiritual and political concerns into daily lives and group practices, having a smaller "carbon footprint," and solving the problem of affordable and more inclusive housing. How can we help these experiments flourish, learn from them, and promote others?

These times demand that all of us have strong internal spiritual resources whatever our particular personal theology. We cannot be resilient or countercultural without them. One of the other arenas where we likely have some work to do is re-examining our operating models of spiritual development. Are they still relevant? Are they sufficiently comprehensive to meet today's context and our understanding of the psychological and spiritual challenges we face? Do we have enough and the right types of programming for Unitarian Universalists of all ages to support the formation and flourishing of the internal resources we need? How well do we understand and make the connection between our own personal growth and processes that bring about larger social change?

Many contemporary psychologists, educators, and religious leaders talk about how disconnected most people in highly industrialized societies are from nature, for example, and how this is a root problem in terms of how we form and live out our values and worldview. Do our Unitarian Universalist models of spiritual development speak to this? Do they speak to how we grow spiritually in our understanding and solidarity with those living in poverty or with those experiencing racism, distinct from growing in our political or social understandings? Are our spiritual development models so abstract as to ignore these dimensions?

Bill Plotkin's writing is very helpful when tackling the question about how to create a culture of resistance as a denomination. He has developed an "eco-soulcentric developmental wheel" that speaks directly to the spiritual tasks and capacities needed to be part of the Great Turning, without relying on any assumptions about God. His model is based on the premise that we in the West, and particularly in the US, live in a "pathologically adolescent" culture. In *Nature and the Human Soul: Cultivating Wholeness and Community in a Fragmented World*, he points out the obvious: "A viable plan for transforming our culture will not come from the worldview or the values that produced it." Instead, we must grow more mature adults and elders to help lead the transformation. Plotkin's model assumes eight stages of spiritual development that are not chronological, but instead are based on having acquired various skills and sensibilities. It posits sequential spiritual tasks to master that have us more authentically and justly engage with other humans as well as the rest of our natural world.

In an interview with Bill Moyers, longtime activist Grace Lee Boggs talked about how revolution and evolution are no longer necessarily in tension. Human evolution is much more than changing human features. It includes evolving human systems such as economies, societies, and political systems. Plotkin and other ecopsychologists, as well as some contemporary theologians, argue that it is important to see the Earth as Gaia—a living system—and that her healing and flourishing depend on our psychospiritual development and maturation. Participating in the world's liberation means taking charge of our own liberation and understanding how that is linked to others nearby and distant from us.

We might strengthen our Coming of Age work with youth through more intense time in nature as well as deeper social justice experiences. We can do more to honor and tap the wisdom of elders and use that in some fresh, meaningful ways to provide support to adults and youth in the work of resistance and transformation. We should offer compelling social justice and spiritual growth experiences in the wilderness and in challenging urban and suburban settings. There is a lot of possibility here for dynamic, engaging, new programming.

The thirteenth-century Sufi mystic and poet Rumi offers twenty-first century Unitarian Universalists some very apt advice: "Yesterday I was clever, so I wanted to change the world. Today I am wise, so I am changing myself." The radical shifts the world needs begin with our own institutional cultural transformation. Rumi also instructs us: "Forget safety. Live where you fear to live. Destroy your reputation. Be notorious." In earlier time periods, Unitarians and Universalists were willing to be notorious. They bucked the status quo, skewered commonly held beliefs, created radical new ventures, and at least once, they potentially bet an entire institution's existence on a justice gamble, when the UUA and Beacon Press published the Pentagon Papers.

Pieces of these five conversations are underway within our movement. At present, they are not necessarily tied together or fully fleshed out. Some imperatives, like speaking more prophetically in the pulpit and in community, could happen immediately. Other aspects will take some time, but that should not deter us. While difficult, accepting the challenge to change offers us ways to make our faith more relevant to the world's needs, more alive for existing members, and potentially more attractive to at least some people who are not formally associated with any particular tradition. The question is: Are we willing to be "notorious" now? To live out our most authentic self as a collective religious community?

TAKING IT FURTHER

Pamela Sparr invites us to consider how siloed justice advocacy can hinder, rather than advance, the pursuit of justice. However, these siloed approaches have been our dominant and historical understanding of justice advocacy. What "silos" are you a part of? As a practical experience of getting out of our own silos, we invite you to find someone in your community who is an advocate for justice on an issue that is not one of your own. Next, meet with this person and invite them to share with you their passion for their issue, without educating or informing them of your own. Simply listen and learn, with an active ear for how that other person's sense of passion and commitment may overlap with your own. How might there be intersections between your different passions?

. . . . .

Those who traveled to Detroit as a part of the Unitarian Universalist Ministry for Earth's Collaboratory in 2014 met with activist Grace Lee Boggs and read her book *The Next American Revolution: Sustainable Activism for the Twenty-First Century*. Read this book with an eye toward intersectionality and how Boggs brought people of disparate interests together in a movement.

KATHLEEN McTIGUE

❖

Learning to Change: Immersion Learning and Climate Justice

I N THE 1980S, the US government was deeply involved in supporting the Contra army against the Sandinistas in Nicaragua. Believing that support for this war was both illegal and immoral, a small group of faith leaders founded Witness for Peace in 1983, and under its auspices began bringing groups of US citizens to Nicaragua to give them a firsthand encounter with the realities of the violence. For six months, I served as one of the long-term volunteers on the ground in Nicaragua, hosting these groups and helping to interpret what they saw and heard. More than thirty years later, I still encounter people who traveled on one of these journeys who tell me that the experience completely changed their understanding, perspective, and actions—and, in some cases, their lives.

There are many ways we absorb new information, but one of the most powerful is through direct experience. Experiential or immersion learning programs bring us face-to-face with a dimension of our reality that we had not known before; they touch not only our intellects but our bodies, hearts, and spirits, in ways that are sometimes quite literally life-changing. We hear firsthand stories and witness for ourselves the reality of people whose lives are very different from ours. We break bread together, work side by side, and absorb the sights, smells, and sounds of a new place and culture. We often gain dramatic insight into our own lives in ways that shape our choices when we return home.

But many of the familiar forms of such firsthand encounters are rife with pitfalls. When we travel on a typical short-term service-learning trip, we move from relative privilege into communities struggling with poverty, oppression, and violence. If we embark on such journeys naively, they can be clumsy attempts to help, offering a feel-good sheen for us as travelers but doing little for the people who host us. At their worst, these excursions can perpetuate the very systems of injustice that caused the problems in the first place.

When experiential journeys are done well, however, they can help participants cross barriers of race, culture, and class and gain insight about where we each stand in the matrices of privilege and power. All human beings view the world through lenses shaped by their own location. When we become aware of these lenses, we learn to hold our stories more lightly in order to hear with clarity the alternative stories that others tell. We see more vividly the ways our political and economic systems leave entire populations in the margins, both within our nation and around the world, and we begin to learn what it can mean to become effective allies to their struggles.

These insights and skills are essential if we are to fully engage the challenges we face with climate change. As we confront the destruction caused by expanding drought, rising oceans, and magnified storms, what we can see with glaring consistency is that the destruction does not fall equally on all populations. Poor communities bear the brunt of the damage and receive the least adequate recovery aid. Even before the storm or the water shortages hit, their members are already suffering from woefully inadequate infrastructure and often from decades of environmental degradation.

If we intend to confront the challenges of climate change through a justice lens, we must be willing to privilege the voices, choices, and needs of these frontline communities most affected. And if we ourselves do not come from these communities, we cannot become effective partners to them simply through an act of will. It takes some deep learning about ourselves, the people with whom we wish to be in solidarity, and some tried and true ways to transcend the boundaries that rise between us.

The Unitarian Universalist College of Social Justice (UUCSJ) has developed a model for experiential learning programs designed to facilitate this deep education for social justice. Founded in 2012 as a joint program of the Unitarian Universalist Association and the Unitarian Universalist Service Committee, the mission of the College is to create experiential learning programs that inspire and sustain faith-based activism for justice. I was hired as the UUCSJ Director at its founding. We consider our model to be a work in progress:

imperfect, evolving, and always open to revision and improve-
ment. Yet there are some common elements we believe to be
essential in helping people become effective agents for change
in the months and years after an immersion program has ended.

*Always work with a partner organization made up of the people
who are directly affected.* There are many organizations that
bring volunteers into poor communities within the US or
abroad who create their own staff and structures on the
ground. This provides the kind of schedule and activities that
we often anticipate and keeps us in our comfort zone doing
exactly what we set out to do: help those less fortunate than
ourselves.

It is a very different encounter and experience when the
partnership is forged with an organization made up of and
directed by the same people who are suffering an injustice. In
this case, we are working directly with people who have taken
some measure of control over their situation. They are in a
position to tell us what they actually need from us, and though
that sometimes feels incongruent with our expectations, we
are far more likely to be of genuine use.

Partnership with an affected community means there is a
pretty good chance that the dynamic will be a two-way street,
despite all the pitfalls that arise from unequal privilege and
power. The basis for the program is framed as one of mutuality, in which the needs and wishes of the partner organization
are primary. When these are congruent with the goals of an
experiential learning program, we move forward; when they
are not, we discuss together, clarify our hopes, and ask new

questions, and the process itself makes clear that the developing relationship is one of mutuality.

In the wake of the catastrophic Haitian earthquake in 2010,
UUSC developed a partnership with a longstanding Haitian
organization focused on land rights and peasant empower-
ment: the Papaye Peasant Movement, or MPP. For four years,
College of Social Justice delegations helped MPP develop an
eco-village model for resettlement of refugees from Port-au-
Prince. But once these villages were completed, we began
rethinking with MPP how the focus for these groups should
shift, based on MPP's core purpose and goals. The programs
are now framed around international dimensions of food sovereignty, a central concern for MPP and its members.

Focus on justice rather than service. Within our congregations,
we often fail to make this distinction. We consider the weekly
meal we offer at the soup kitchen in the same realm as advocacy at the state capitol for supportive housing, or protesting
unfair wages. Both are valuable and necessary, but they are not
the same: One activity helps people with an immediate and
chronic need, and the other seeks to challenge and change the
systems that give rise to that need in the first place.

The distinction is particularly important if we travel from
our own community into another for a learning program.
Because of our own deep desire to be of use, it can feel very
gratifying to fly into a community, spend a week of hard labor,
and see a new home going up or the walls of a schoolhouse
finished. We head back home feeling that we've done something specific, concrete, and useful.

But the hard truth is that the people who live and work full-time in these communities are far more competent at the art of construction than our motley collection of amateurs. What they need from us is likely to be less tangible and satisfying to us as the visitors, but much more congruent with the call of justice. They need us to listen to their stories and bear witness to their struggles and victories; to hear and honor the solutions they choose for themselves; to look unflinchingly at the historic, systemic injustices that may continue to benefit us today; and to go home prepared to roll up our sleeves and tackle those systems.

This work for justice back home is the only "service" component in many of our journeys. With the Lummi Nation in Washington State, for instance, the most pressing issue within their community has been the campaign to prevent a coal terminal from being built on traditional tribal fishing grounds. The historic victory that was delivered in the spring of 2016, in which a study by the US Army Corps of Engineers concluded that the terminal would violate treaty rights, came about in part because of the broad alliances Lummi activists had forged with non-native allies all over the United States.

Use a study framework before, during, and after the program. It is remarkable how often a service-learning program is offered without any expectation that participants will prepare themselves beyond reviewing a packing list. When we travel into unfamiliar territory, we owe it to both the host community and ourselves to do some learning in advance—whether we're going to post-hurricane Brooklyn or to a small village in

India. In order to make sense of the struggles we witness, we owe it to our host communities to put in the time and energy to learn all that we can about the background context before we travel.

At a bare minimum, we should study the history of the country or area; learn about the economic and racial inequalities and their roots; and when it's a foreign country, study the history and legacy of colonialism. At least some of what we read or view should be from the perspective of those who live in the community. We should know how our host organization was founded, how it engages its work of justice, and what role it plays in the service-learning journey.

Though it may not be quite as obvious, it is just as important for us to study ourselves in the context of the journey and justice issue. This kind of self-study helps us to understand our own position in the complicated and entwined matrices of privilege and power. It makes us more aware of the particular lenses through which we view the world and helps us remember that our own slant on things is not the only way to see. It makes us more mindful of our personal preferences and expectations, and this in turn allows us to hold them more lightly, so we can be open and flexible to whatever the experience might bring us.

Continuing our study after we return home integrates our brief, intense immersion into our "regular" lives. It helps us consider how we have been changed. It also helps us grapple with where we are called to engage with institutional injustice that is either directly or indirectly linked to what we have experienced. In the 1980s, the Witness for Peace immersion experience galvanized people to new or deeper efforts to end US involvement in the Nicaraguan war. In our current era, the UUCSJ Border Immersion journey to Arizona and Mexico creates the same powerful determination to work for immigration justice. Even when lines of connection from experience to action are less clear, this post-program time is a pivotal opportunity to reinforce our learning by engaging in action.

Ground the program and participants in reflection and spiritual practices. When we take on a practice of prayer or meditation that quiets down the inner noise of our minds, we can be less reactive when things don't go according to schedule, more open to seeing and hearing new things, and more gentle with ourselves, our hosts, and our fellow participants. Likewise, the opportunity for group reflection makes room for new insight and for the collective wisdom to emerge.

When we travel into a place in which the suffering caused by poverty and environmental degradation is obvious and chronic, our spiritual practices support us in another way: They help us to bear witness. When we first see the stark contrast between the hardships in our host community and our own comfortable lifestyles, we can be flooded not only with sympathy and compassion, but with guilt, anxiety, shame, and anger. These feelings are important teachers, and they can lead us to make significant and far-reaching changes in our lives— but only if we are willing to stay with our own discomfort long enough to gain new understanding and determination.

No one enjoys painful feelings when they arise, so we have many strategies for avoiding them. One of the most common within the realm of experiential learning is to leap into "fix-it" mode: We come up with a great idea that will surely make things better, like a scholarship program or a solar lamp project. As well-meaning as these ideas may be, if they spring from our own need to be of use and are not rooted in the wisdom of the host community, they are likely to have unintended negative results.

Spiritual practices can keep us aware of our own motives. They help us bear witness to the reality around us—to see its causes and true scope—and to our own uncomfortable feelings. Staying present this way allows us to know the people of the community not as helpless victims in need of our schemes, but as people with agency, dignity, and their own ideas for change. Staying present to our feelings of unease in the face of gross inequality also allows us to channel those feelings into passionate, grounded, and effective campaigns for change within our own spheres of influence.

Immersion learning, done well, can spark or renew our passion for justice and give us fresh insight into our own capacity for action. As we come to know more dimensions of our immense, complex web of life, we also realize more fully the truth that a tug on just one of its strands affects the whole web. When we consider the term "service-learning program" in this context, we realize that the most effective service we can render is the continuing work for justice right where we are rooted, newly open to the ways each action can ripple out far beyond what our limited vision can perceive. The arc of our universe is indeed long; each of our small efforts help bend it toward justice.

TAKING IT FURTHER

The UU College of Social Justice has multiple opportunities to engage in experiential learning, justice-oriented trips. Review the possibilities listed here: www.uucsj.org/journeys/#trips. Might you or your community be interested in engaging in such a firsthand experience?

. . . . .

As another option, consider working with local partners, agencies, or activists in creating a firsthand opportunity to learn about and be in relationship with a community affected by environmental and racial justice issues. Can you create a one-day "immersion" experience, a collaborative visit to a local community that is not your own, that deepens understanding and helps build relationship with that community?

PEGGY CLARKE

❖

Eating the Earth

I N 2006, my friend Judy sent an email to a small circle, offering us her farm share while she was out of town for the upcoming three weeks. The first week was mine. I drove up to Cascade Farm on a sunny July afternoon. I parked on their unpaved road and followed the chickens to a big, open barn. Inside there were tables, each heavy with wood crates filled with the week's harvest and signs letting me know what to do. "Please take one pound of kale; four cucumbers; three pounds potatoes; two eggplants; one bunch each of parsley, basil, oregano, tarragon; as many hot peppers as you'd like; six summer squash; a half pound of chard; two heads romaine; one pound pole beans."

When I got home, I called some friends and told them there's no way my family could eat all this food, so they came over that evening to share a meal with us on the deck. We spent the evening drinking cold tea, singing (that happens a lot when we're all together), and eating the gift of the earth.

The next year, we all joined Cascade Farm. We traveled to the farm on Thursday afternoons to collect our harvest. We left notes for each other on the sign-in sheets, emailed recipe ideas when we got home, and shared meals, often impromptu. Our summer was filled with friends and music and fresh food. The summer after, we asked another friend to teach us how to preserve this gorgeous harvest. We spent afternoons in each other's kitchens, practicing the art of canning. I prepared jams and jellies, filled freezer bags with carrots, onions, spinach, and zucchini, cooked big pots of Portuguese kale soup and trays of spinach pie, and lined my shelves with chutneys and salsas.

In 2008, I was a member of The Junior League and was asked to chair its Signature Project Committee. We were given a general direction and told to create something that would define the group for the next decade. We focused on intergenerational work, after an extensive research process. I accepted the direction along with the enthusiasm of my co-chair and a committee made up of what the organization considered its finest volunteers. Some of what energized this group was the opportunity to play a role in an esteemed and proud history, and we were charged with figuring out what's next.

We discovered quickly that in an age-segregated culture like ours, generational integration is becoming a critical issue. While my parents were raised in neighborhoods with people of many generations interacting, so many of us live in cocoons, surrounded by people no more than a few years older or younger than ourselves. Our children spend their days segregated by age, even playing team sports on weekends with children in their own grade instead of in multi-age groups. There are very few places left where communities live across generational lines. As we started to design our options, we continued to come around to my experience at Cascade Farm. I held up the farm as one of the few places left where people of all ages and cultures can engage fully and where community has in our past and will in our future be sustained and supported. My co-chair liked my ideas about a communal place for people to grow their own food, but it wasn't until she returned from a vacation in Greece that she was committed. When she got home, she called immediately to tell me about harvest time on this tiny island where she and her family stayed. "They don't have fresh water," she exclaimed, "but they have spectacular gardens!" Every morning, she and her husband and four kids joined local families to gather their food from the grounds. They'd walk back to their rented house, arms filled with the day's harvest. She talked about how excited each kid got, eating bush beans on the path home. The people in this little Greek village share rain barrels and take turns watering the garden. Everyone participates in the growing of the town food—children of every age, young adults, parents, elders—everyone pitches in, has a task or shares a task with their neighbors. This family connected to Earth, to their food, to their new community, and to each other because of those gardens. They had been transformed.

My co-chair, Roseann, was interested in intergenerational work as the only reasonable model for social sustainability. The fragmentation of American culture into specific, age-segregated groups has been disconcerting to her, and her experience in those Greek gardens demonstrated a more traditional and healthier way for families to live and be in relationship. Rather than parsing out tasks for a single person, planting, watering, weeding, and harvesting with others in the community deepened ties across generational lines. Multigenerational living offers rich opportunities for relationships and may even become necessary as we reimagine ways of living together on our fragile planet in response to our current climate crisis. In light of consistent reports of isolation from every corner of American culture, participating in life-sustaining, communal, multigenerational activities that deepen our connection to Earth could become a healing balm.

With that hope, Roseann and I created InterGenerate, a small food-justice organization. Our original idea was to build intentional community around an organic garden in which people across a variety of diversities grow their own food. We designed a model that allowed us to keep the membership cost to $50 or less each year, making it financially accessible, with an additional commitment to shared work and communal engagement. We opened our first community garden in Mt. Kisco, New York, during the spring of 2010, in addition to a teaching garden at John Jay Homestead, a state-owned historic site. In 2012 we opened two more gardens and launched a successful experiment of communal caretaking for about forty-five chickens with twenty-five households.

Community gardening provides equal access to food that's good, clean, and fair at very lost cost. Growing our produce locally creates greater food security, and doing it organically, as is common in community gardens, reduces risks associated with pesticides and other agricultural chemicals. Local sourcing also has a dramatic impact on reducing our nation's carbon footprint, as 18–30 percent of the carbon being sent into our atmosphere is a direct result of agri-business and agricultural transportation.

Until recently, the United States was the breadbasket of the world, able to sustain our population. Today, we are a net food importer, suddenly dependent on large corporations for our food supply, often turning a blind eye to the human cost paid across the system, from migrant workers and farm hands to supermarket cashiers. In addition, we are generally uninterested in the price the planet is paying for transporting all that food or in the suffering animals experience as we devalue their lives to keep the cost of food down in the corporate assembly line.

When I buy bananas here in New York, it's so easy to forget all the parts of the food chain that provide me that nineteen-cent banana. But forgetting doesn't absolve me of my accountability. I am accountable to the farm workers who picked those bananas, earning less than a living wage for one of five major corporations that harvest bananas for US consumption. I'm accountable to the women who drop those bananas into vats of cancer-causing chemicals to slow the ripening. When I buy a banana for nineteen cents, I'm accountable to those women when they get sick from those chemicals and have no health care. I'm accountable to the children they leave behind. I'm accountable to the workers who get those green bananas in boxes and those who drive the trucks. I'm accountable to the children in the neighborhoods those diesel trucks drive through each day on their way to deliver those bananas. I'm accountable for polluted air and the burning of fossil fuels and the carbon that is overheating the Earth. I'm accountable to the trees that were felled, the habitats lost, the animals who died to clear land to make room for the supermarket where I shop, and for the parking lot hundreds of cars drive into every day to buy those bananas. I'm not responsible for every piece of this system, but as part of the system, as the end goal of the system—which is to sell to the consumer—I am accountable for how food gets to my plate.

Community gardens and supporting local, independent farms address these justice issues by creating the possibility of having food that's financially accessible while working the land or being connected to those who work it, who are also our neighbors. These practices also ensure the humane treatment of animals and use natural growing practices that help us live gently on the Earth. In addition, community gardens build and strengthen communities across diversities that usually divide us. Food is a human need regardless of gender identity, age, class, physical ability, sexual orientation, race, country of origin, religion, or any of the other identities that have traditionally segregated us in American culture. Community gardens become the framework for people to work toward shared ends in unison and without barriers.

Environmental justice requires us to ask the question, "Who reaps the benefit and who bears the burden of the modern industrial society?" Too often it's people of color and the poor who bear the burden while white, wealthy people reap the benefit. Local food sourcing is an equalizer.

It isn't important how many pounds of food we've grown at InterGenerate or how many suppers we've shared or how many eggs we've harvested or even the exact number of members we have. What matters is how many friends we've made and how many times I've seen my son run through the fields with other garden children or lie in the grass with the chickens. What matters is the afternoon Jodi and I knelt for hours thinning beets, and the cuts and scrapes on my arms after filling the compost pile with Li Lai, and the pictures Marion posted when she got her first strawberry to grow. I can easily recall how delicately two sisters nursed some milkweed others were clearing and how we all gathered to watch the snapping turtles climb our fences when they realized we'd blocked their path. I vividly remember the time in our first garden, where I did not have a plot, a woman in her eighties gave me her first head of lettuce as a thank-you for opening that garden. I remember the young couple who finally felt at home in their new town, and the email I received at the end of our first season from a woman who said that our garden brought her back to life. They were transformed.

A member of my congregation was inspired a few years ago to start a community garden. It's open to congregants and community members who want or need to grow their own food. I've also become a coach for the Green Sanctuary program for congregations looking to make sustainable food a part of what they do. I've been wondering what it would mean if congregations grew the food we use for the variety of feeding programs in which we participate. What if the breakfasts and dinners we packed were planted, watered, weeded, and harvested by our own hands on our own property? What if that were true of the food we serve on Sunday mornings? Or for pot lucks? What if we spent our springs and summers and falls welcoming the stranger, welcoming families willing and able to grow their own food, who are completely unfamiliar to us. Maybe they don't look like us or have different family histories or educational backgrounds or they speak different languages. What would it be like if people in our communities thought of our churches as places people gather for harvest suppers and to learn the arts of canning and drying and freezing and preserving, places that welcome all people seeking to live gently on Earth and with each other? Would that be transformational?

Carbon levels in our atmosphere are catastrophic. If we aren't looking for transformation now, when would we start? Scientists tell us that we need to leave 80 percent of detected fossil fuels in the ground, even while corporations are funding searches for new reserves. The current crisis requires altering our infrastructure dramatically and quickly so that ideally in the next ten years, we convert everything that is oil, gas, or coal powered such that it can be fueled by renewable sources. Continuing our current course of action is immoral and will ultimately lead to Earth's inability to maintain human life. And while that's happening to all of us, communities of color are most affected today, while generations unborn are poised to suffer from our inaction.

The point of InterGenerate—and of many community, communal, and urban gardens—is to create the possibility for equal access to food that's good, clean, and fair. Membership fees are low, and are waived, if needed. Gardens are open from sunrise to sunset seven days a week. Community gardens are a good way to welcome immigrants, especially those from rural/agricultural backgrounds. In a garden setting, they have the opportunity to become the teachers, often feeling more at home than anywhere else in their new country. In addition to creating an empowering situation socially, community gardens also create food security for many who are marginalized, such as the elderly, and low-income and immigrant populations.

The current interest in community gardens began with LaDonna Redmund, on the West Side of Chicago, when her two-year-old son was diagnosed with severe allergies. Because there was no organic food in her neighborhood, her only option was to take two buses (with two kids in tow) across the city, where she could find whole, pesticide-free food, but at a very high price. In desperation, she reclaimed land around her home, ultimately expanding to alleyways and rooftops, creating an urban farm and the possibility of self-determination for all the families in her neighborhood.

If we are going to survive this dangerous time, it will be because we are open to transformation. It will be because we are able to envision new ways of living together, new ways of being in relationship with the Earth. While we consider things like growing our own food to be a "new way," it is, in fact, the old way. It's how humans have survived for thousands of years. Sometimes critics suggest that community gardens are elitist. That comment only demonstrates how distant we've become from the sources of our food. Food security is at the core of self-sufficiency, and for historically marginalized communities, it is a necessary part of self-determination.

We are good people on a dying planet. We think a lot and talk a lot and mean very well. We want to do what's right but sometimes our desire doesn't translate into action and often we're so busy with the details of our own existence we just can't think about anything outside of the next few hours. We want stronger communities and a healthier planet. But we don't have time even to learn about all the things we have to do to get there, so we hope someone else will do enough for the rest of us. I speak here for myself, without pointing fingers. I don't do as much as I wish. Sometimes I don't do half enough. Sometimes I'm embarrassed not to be doing more. I think I'll start this or that as soon as I have the time or the money. . . .

But, that's how we got here. Good people not being able to get past the inertia of our individual lives. We who have churches or other faith communities have more than most. We have each other. We aren't talking about individual lives, we're talking about our collective life, the life we share as a congregation.

In our churches we can make real changes. We can decide together to think differently, to act differently, to live differently. Houses of worship are centers of hope. In churches and synagogues and mosques and temples the world around, people are introduced to the possibilities of the human experience. In these places, people reach beyond themselves into the depth of community and the depth of the spiritual and return to their lives knowing we can be more.

This essay is about food, but it's also about harvesting a deeper way of living. It's about planting and watering and weeding and harvesting community. It's about deeper life, better life, shared life.

It's about being transformed.

TAKING IT FURTHER

Peggy Clarke explains how some communities may not have easy or affordable access to fresh fruits and vegetables and other healthy food options, locations often referred to as "food deserts." What food deserts may exist near where you live? (Try Googling "food desert maps.")

. . . . .

How might you learn more about the food chains of which we are a part? Which populations actively farm the fruits, vegetables, and other farm products that we enjoy? To learn more about migrant farm workers and their role in our food chain, visit this website: https://tinyurl.com/y9mqks9t.

. . . . .

How might greater awareness of our food chain, and the populations that support it, invite compassion, love, and engagement? How could you and/or your community bring these virtues more fully alive in your interactions with individuals who work in our food and restaurant industries?

MEL HOOVER AND ROSE EDINGTON

❖

Water Unites Us

B EFORE THE WATER CRISIS in Flint, Michigan, another
water crisis affected the communities in and around
Charleston, West Virginia, where we served as ministers. Unfortunately, we recognize that these water crises will likely not be
the last ones our nation must grapple with, given the ongoing
reality of environmental degradation and the unpredictable
impacts of climate change. This essay describes the local community organizing and humanitarian work of the Unitarian
Universalist Congregation of Charleston, West Virginia (UUC),
in the hope that sharing this experience will be helpful to those
who find themselves navigating similar crises.

Historically and currently, fossil fuel corporations and their
accompanying industries have been eager to exploit the environment and labor to increase their net worth and to influence legislation to their benefit. Often, people must work for
the very companies that destroy the places they hold most
dear. In West Virginia, this has led to a kind of "Appalachian
fatalism," reinforced by what seems like a "disaster du jour,"
which leaves many citizens with a mixture of resignation and
resilience.

Members of the Charleston congregation responded with resilience and direct action to two such disasters: first, when Freedom Industries and the West Virginia American Water Company (WVAW) allowed 4-methylcyclohexanemethanol (MCHM) to poison a water system serving 300,000 people in nine counties of the greater Kanawha Valley in January 2014; and second, when severe flooding occurred in some of the same counties and surrounding areas in June 2016.

Since the local emergency response system was not activated, notification about the chemical spill and water crisis was somewhat patchwork. Mel had just quenched his thirst with a tall glass of tap water when the phone rang. It was Rose's mom checking to see if we'd heard the breaking news: We were to stop using tap water for anything other than flushing the toilet or putting out fires. The usual advisories to boil the water to clean it would not suffice. Not everyone heard the initial radio and TV announcements. But everyone noticed an unusual licorice smell in the air, which turned out to be an alert that crude MCHM was in our water.

MCHM is a foaming agent used to "clean" clay and shale from coal so it can be burned to generate electricity. Not intended for human contact, the only regulatory guidelines for its toxicity applied to rats. To determine nontoxic levels for human exposure, Eastman Chemical and the US Centers for Disease Control conducted a study in which they took the amount of MCHM that would kill a rat and extrapolated from that figure to determine how many parts per billion in the water would be safe for the average male human body. This figure was then used to set the standard for when our poisoned water would be safe for drinking, cooking, and showering. Pregnant women were advised to not drink the water until MCHM became undetectable.

Adding to the crisis were WVAW's slow response and poor infrastructure. The company chose not to turn off the intake valves in the Elk River, the public's tap water source. WVAW erroneously thought its filters could remove the MCHM, not realizing that the total amount spilled was 10,000 gallons. Although state law mandates that WVAW have a two-day supply of water on hand for emergencies, the backup tanks were empty.

Following the spill, simple acts became complicated. For example, the day after the spill we hosted a worship associate dinner meeting. We were preparing to retire as co-ministers in a few weeks and this would be our last meeting with the worship associates to thank them and work out a schedule for Tricia Hart, the incoming interim minister. Since we could not turn on the tap, we washed potatoes with bottled water, baked them, and provided a variety of toppings, washed down with beer and wine.

We could not move the meeting to a restaurant. The Kanawha-Charleston Health Department had ordered all restaurants closed until the tap water was declared safe or owners could demonstrate they had enough bottled water on hand to operate. Restaurant owners had to wonder if they should invest in a filter system, purchase gallons of bottled water, or wait it out, not knowing how long it would be. Some went out of business. Hourly workers with little or no financial cushion suddenly found themselves without an income for an indefinite period of time. Parents had to scramble for childcare because all schools were closed.

Rose contacted the Baptist church of her childhood, located in a nearby town with a water source separate from WVAW, and was able to fill large coolers with safe water for use at UUC and at home. On her way to get the water, she passed what looked like miles of cars lined up at stores to buy bottled water because the state had not yet set up water distribution sites. She felt so thankful to have a place where she could fill the coolers. We didn't realize how important it would be just to have the usual coffee hour at our congregation on the Sunday after the spill, but as one member so aptly put it, "We've all been traumatized, and we needed something this normal."

In the aftermath of this ecological travesty and the ensuing trauma, UUC was called to minister within the congregation and to the community at large: helping low-income families who otherwise would have to choose between purchasing bottled water and paying their rent, delivering water to those who could not get to distribution sites, and organizing and advocating for legislation to ensure safe water.

UUC responded well to this crisis, and to the flood in 2016, for several reasons:

- *The congregation had a long-standing activist reputation.* Well before we arrived as co-ministers in September 2002, we knew of various members' involvement in justice causes: attending and advocating at legislative hearings, standing up for reproductive freedom, keeping textbooks with scientific truths from being banned, and sponsoring two Bosnian refugee families. One of our first tasks was to encourage UUC members to publicly claim Unitarian Universalism as an expression of their activism. In 2007, Charleston City Council member and Unitarian Universalist Marc Weintraub did so, successfully introducing a nondiscrimination in employment and housing bill for LGBT folks. Unitarian Universalists crowded city council chambers on the joyful night his bill passed.

- *The UUC building was seen as a safe space for community meetings.* Church member Kathryn Stone was like a one-woman social justice committee. She encouraged UUC to practice a ministry of hospitality to justice groups whose controversial positions might make finding meeting space difficult. During our candidating week she arranged for representatives from environmental justice groups to orient us on issues of mountaintop removal mining and the colonizing effects of corporate power in the state. As conversations among us deepened, the idea emerged, and was immediately embraced, of working more closely together. It was decided to form the Friends of the Mountains coalition, as a counter to the corporate-sponsored Friends of Coal.

    After the chemical spill, the greater community initially needed a gathering place to share fears and concerns, and then to organize for safe water. UUC was a known, trusted place for everyone across race, class, age, and gender to come together, so it was a natural site to welcome emerging and longtime justice groups and concerned citizens.

From an organizing standpoint, the chemical spill was timely. The West Virginia legislative session had just begun when the lack of water forced it to adjourn. Legislators could not stay in hotels or eat or work at the capitol for nearly the first quarter of the session.

When the governor called stakeholders together to draft legislation to address the spill, he neglected to include citizen or environmental justice groups. He only invited representatives of corporations and industries. By this time, directly affected citizens, who had not previously seen themselves as activists, had formed several organizations, including the West Virginia Safe Water Roundtable, Advocates for a Safe Water System, and a small business leaders group. These groups, along with more established environmental justice groups, protested their exclusion. This time, industry would not get to write the law behind closed doors—the community showed up every day of the remaining session to advocate for safe water. It mattered that the media supported citizen efforts and ensured that accurate information was commonly shared.

Rallies, demonstrations, and press conferences were often planned at UUC and attended by UUC members. It all paid off when legislation was passed that required chemical storage tanks to be registered and monitored.

• *The congregation embraced mutual ministry.* During our co-ministry, we didn't want the congregation to fall into the social justice-versus-spirituality divide. To us, they are two sides of the same coin. We reminded the congregation that all of us are engaged in mutual ministry and in one way or another are involved in justice issues. If members weren't out advocating, demonstrating, and attending meetings, their support in other ways helped those who were. Their pledges help us open the building to social justice organizations and causes. Their caring and compassion for one another build up the community of support for all the ministries that call us. Together, all help answer the question: What is the purpose of our congregation?

- *UUC appreciates professional ministry and also understands that the congregation is greater than its ministers.* UUC began in 1953 as part of the lay-led fellowship movement. Even as it grew to support professional ministry, it has always valued its lay leadership, as do we. One of the last tasks the UUC board asked of us, its co-ministers, was to give them suggestions about where to direct the funds that were coming in from Unitarian Universalists near and far to help with the water crisis. We made our recommendations and turned them over to the board and incoming interim minister.

Everyone had growing edges in dealing with this crisis, personally and as UUC members. Board members wondered if it was appropriate to receive money to help with this crisis. The answer was yes—not only was it a way for people near and far to express their help and support, it also enhanced the congregation's ministry. The experience also taught us that funds need to be dealt with responsibly and with transparency.

The board established a Clean Water Fund and a Clean Water Task Force to administer the financial donations. The interim minister served as an ex-officio member, the membership was chosen by the congregation, and a separate account for the funds was set up by the treasurer.

More than $24,000 came in as individual gifts and from Unitarian Universalist congregations in our region and nationally. The task force invited UUC members to suggest grant recipients, keeping in mind these purposes:

- *Direct service*: getting clean water to those who need it
- *Education and research*: supporting those who are learning and teaching about the effects of the spill, and spreading awareness and interest in and beyond West Virginia
- *Advocacy*: challenging local and federal government officials and agencies to change policies to better protect water sources now and in the future

A number of examples demonstrate the effectiveness of the fund. The Keeper of the Mountains Foundation and the West Virginia Clean Water Hub reached out to those seemingly forgotten in the crisis—those disabled or in rural areas, far from water distribution centers—to get clean water to those most in need. The Hub's long-term plan is to develop rainwater catchment systems in these areas so water will always be available.

The West Virginia Rivers Coalition produced the documentary *Elk River Blues*, which covers the Elk's history from its "discovery" by Europeans to the present, from its headwaters to the site of the chemical spill and its eventual joining with the Kanawha River. This film not only educates, it provides fodder for advocacy. In his retirement, filmmaker and Unitarian Universalist Mike Youngren became a volunteer video director for nonprofits as his commitment to disseminating social justice messages, including *Elk River Blues*. The number of local, national, and international clicks to its website document its widespread effect.

The Clean Water Fund and Task Force were still in operation when the June 2016 floods occurred, so the congregation was immediately prepared to help. UUC became an emergency supply collection and distribution point, coordinated by UUC's operations coordinator, Paul Dalzell. He oversaw the delivery of four truckloads of supplies to flooded areas within twenty-four hours. An elected delegate from UUC, supported by UU Ministry for Earth and MelRose Ministries (which provides consulting and advocacy on issues of intersectionality), he enhanced appeals for funds with up-to-the-minute flood reports and networking during General Assembly 2016.

Again, funds came in from generous Unitarian Universalists and others. Because UUC had a structure in place and a track record of successfully distributing funds where they are most needed, the Unitarian Universalist Service Committee provided a grant in 2016.

As of April 2017 a tentative legal settlement was reached between West Virginia American Water and Eastman Chemical Company awarding $151 million to those households and businesses affected by the spill. US District Court Judge

Copenhaver, who has stated that the legal fees are too high, will okay the release of funds as soon as legal fees are determined. A series of articles on the settlement can be found through an Internet search, using the phrase "West Virginia American water settlement."

The Clean Water Task Force will now look for ways to help beyond FEMA and other governmental outreach by finding those who fall through the cracks. The overall plan, as described on the UUC website, is to put "Unitarian Universalist values to work, making sure that help reaches those who need it most, as well as supporting initiatives that focus on understanding what made this disaster so devastating, and how our state might be better prepared in the future. The Task Force will solicit grant applications from non-profits working in the areas of direct relief, education/research, and advocacy. After reviewing applications and interviewing applicants, the Task Force will recommend specific grants to the UUC Board for approval."

One of the greatest lessons from these experiences is that water everywhere is at risk, that everyone is downstream from something, and nearly everyone is at potential risk from flooding. According to a National Climate Assessment report cited in *USA Today* in August 2016, heavy rain events increased by 71 percent between 1958 and 2013. Increases are greatest in the Northeast and Midwest; however, increases in extreme water events are projected for all US regions.

Threats to clean water are becoming West Virginia's new canary in the cage. The metaphor refers to the canaries coal miners took into the mines to monitor for poisonous gas. The canary's death or lack of chirping warned miners to get out before the gas accumulated enough to deprive them of oxygen or cause an explosion.

The canaries in West Virginia today are usually communities of low-income people of color dealing with new water challenges on top of the existing challenges of clear-cut timbering, mountaintop removal mining, and fracking. Sometimes we feel that the entire state—its people and its land—is becoming a canary, seen as marginal. Be warned that what affects the marginalized, if left unchecked, will eventually affect everyone. We encourage Unitarian Universalist congregations to be aware of their local "canaries" and to prepare kind and just ways to be in partnership with them before, during, and after crises.

These words, taken from the prayer we gave at the vigil on the first anniversary of the chemical spill, encapsulate our learnings:

Water unites us! All water is one water, shape-shifting as it goes on and on in its unending cycle. The stream we gather by tonight unites us with all the waters of the world, and all the life of the world, for all of life depends on water. And that is why this common, everyday element on which our very lives depend is sacred. In our thankfulness for water, let us remember to honor, cherish, and care for it—for our own lives, for all life touched by water, and for those who come after us.

TAKING IT FURTHER

Mel Hoover and Rose Edington discuss local water contamination issues. Where does your water supply come from? Where are potentially polluting industries and water treatment facilities located in relationship to where you live? Who lives where those industries are located?

. . . . .

Are there neighborhoods in your community that have lead pipes in them? Are there populations near you that are drinking contaminated water of any kind? Why might such circumstances exist and what can be done about them? Visit this interactive website to learn more about lead exposure where you live: vox.com/a/lead -exposure-risk-map.

DEBORAH J. CRUZ, WITH ALEX KAPITAN

❖

The Journey of Partnering for Justice

If you have come here to help me, you are wasting your time. But if you have come because your liberation is bound up with mine, then let us work together.

—LILLA WATSON, Australian aboriginal elder, activist, and educator

IN MAY 2016, something truly remarkable happened. The Indigenous communities of the Salish Sea—the intricate network of coastal waterways in the Pacific Northwest that includes what settlers call Puget Sound—experienced an unprecedented first-stage win in a long battle to keep the largest coal export facility in North America from being built on their sacred lands and waters.

Xwe'chi'eXen, also known as Cherry Point, is a beautiful stretch of coastline within the Salish Sea, a sixty-mile journey south by canoe from Vancouver, British Columbia, and a hundred-mile journey north from Seattle, Washington. It is home to many endangered and threatened wildlife species, including Chinook salmon, southern resident orca whales,

Puget Sound steelhead, Steller sea lions, humpback whales, leatherback sea turtles, marbled murrelets, and spotted frogs. Xwe'chi'eXen is also the site of an ancient burial ground and an ancestral village of the Lummi Nation dating back 175 generations. Lummi Nation's way of life has evolved around these waters, always maintaining an enduring connection from today's reality to that of their ancestors hundreds of years ago.

Unfortunately, the Salish Sea area, Cherry Point in particular, is viewed as a lucrative industrial zone, and is dominated by British Petroleum, Intalco, and ConocoPhillips—companies that have already had devastating environmental impacts on the fragile ecosystem. If the proposed Gateway Pacific Terminal were to be built, there is no question that the consequences would be disastrous. However, after years of organizing and activism led by Lummi Nation, the US Army Corps of Engineers ruled that the potential impacts of the proposed facility on the Lummi's historic territory and treaty-guaranteed fishing rights could not be mitigated, and denied the permit.

Lummi Nation wasn't alone in its historic struggle to fight for the survival of its ancient lands and waters and its *sche'lang'en* (way of life). Nor were they alone in fighting for the ecosystem of the Salish Sea and, truly, our global ecosystem. The Bellingham Unitarian Fellowship was there with them, fighting side by side and hand in hand, partners in the struggle.

The story of the partnership between Bellingham Unitarian Fellowship (BUF) and Lummi Nation started with a single person. When Beth Brownfield moved to Bellingham, Washington, in 2004, she brought a passion and two decades of experience in Indigenous rights activism. She quickly realized that although her new hometown sat across Bellingham Bay from Lummi Nation and only thirty miles down the road from the Nooksack Indian Tribe, few Bellingham residents had any knowledge of their Indigenous neighbors.

So she started facilitating classes at a local Academy for Lifelong Learning on Indigenous history and present-day culture, visiting the Lummi and Nooksack Nations for permission to teach about the local tribes' history and culture, since she is not of that background, and to connect with potential presenters. Because of the relationships she formed, in 2006 she learned that Lummi Nation was hosting the 2007 Tribal Canoe Journey, an important annual event for Pacific Northwest native peoples, focused on the recovery and preservation of culture, traditional knowledge, and spirituality. Up to 60,000 people were expected to participate, and Lummi Nation would feed 5,000 of them breakfast and dinner for six days. No one in Bellingham or the Whatcom County government was aware of the upcoming event, so she asked her Lummi contacts if she could help and received an enthusiastic yes. Beth turned to her congregation, and a small group of people volunteered to help. For the next six months they met weekly with the Lummi Canoe Journey planning committee to find out specific needs they could assist with. They scoured the county for volunteers, funds, food donations, and other services, assisting in securing between $60,000 and $80,000 in cash, goods, and services. This included engaging the mayor of Bellingham to host a celebration to honor Lummi Nation. For the first time, Coast Salish nations and peoples were officially acknowledged by government officials as the original inhabitants of the area's lands and waters. More than 10,000 people attended the landings of the canoes, and hundreds of volunteers from throughout the county worked over the next six days doing whatever was called for, such as cooking, directing traffic, picking up trash, and passing out water.

The Canoe Journey provided a groundbreaking opportunity for the wider community to get to know their Indigenous neighbors and show their solidarity. Stereotypes were shattered on both sides, friendships made, and experiences shared. The unprecedented outpouring of support came as a surprise to Lummi Nation and other original nations. It opened doors for greater engagement between Whatcom County and Lummi Nation, all because of one person's relationships, developed over the course of years; one congregation's answer to a challenge and dedication to seeing it through; and the simple question: "How can we be of service?"

After the powerful experience of supporting the Tribal Canoe Journey, a small group of BUF members decided to form a congregational ministry team to support native events and issues and maintain their partnership with Lummi Nation. The newly named Native American Connections Committee (NACC) began holding regular educational, spiritual, and justice events and actions for the congregation and the larger community. These included Sunday services with native themes and speakers, observing Native American Heritage Day the day after Thanksgiving, a special Sunday collection for an Indigenous non-profit at least once a year, quarterly food collections for the Lummi Food Bank, and a regional roundup of native events and issues emailed regularly to more than 500 people. NACC also collaborated with Lummi members on a series of community festivals celebrating Coast Salish nations and peoples, and participated in a national Mennonite-sponsored effort to repatriate unidentified ancestral Indigenous remains. In addition, the committee sent BUF members to regional and national events, including a grassroots conference on environmental justice on the Nez Perce Reservation and a UU United Nations spring seminar on Indigenous rights in New York City, both held in 2014.

NACC also recognized the need and possibilities for reaching out to other Unitarian Universalists regarding Indigenous rights. The members resolved to call for the repudiation of the Doctrine of Discovery—a principle that has provided the justification and legal basis for violence against Indigenous peoples because they are non-Christian for more than five centuries. BUF members reached out to every Unitarian Universalist congregation in the Pacific Northwest District, as well as the UUA president and Board of Trustees. These efforts, joined with the efforts of others, led the entire denomination to engage in deep discussion and pass a resolution repudiating the Doctrine of Discovery at the 2012 General Assembly.

Meanwhile, a single event started a chain reaction that no one could have anticipated. In 2010, SSA Marine submitted an expanded permit application to build the Gateway Pacific Terminal at Cherry Point for exporting coal. BUF's Green Sanctuary Committee immediately opposed the project and began working with environmental groups and other faith communities to rally a faith-based response. They teamed up with Earth Ministry, Washington's Interfaith Power and Light chapter, to hold an interfaith educational forum in August 2012, where Lummi Nation Hereditary Chief Tsi'li'xw Bill James was a speaker. He discussed the impact the terminal would have on Lummi Nation, speaking to the cultural and historical significance of the lands and waters of Xwe'chi'eXen, as well as the potential destruction of the Lummi way of life posed by the terminal's threat to their fishing grounds. He challenged the faith communities to change. He called on them to move from their history of inflicting trauma on Indigenous peoples to building bridges of healing, to move from past ambivalence to active support and participation. In the following months, BUF's Green Sanctuary Committee and NACC threw themselves into the struggle. The Green Sanctuary Committee organized and hosted four community educational forums on the aquatic, health, climate, and economic impacts of the proposed terminal. In April 2013, Lummi leaders reached out to NACC for help in bringing the Lummi message to the rest of Whatcom County, especially its faith community. BUF members helped organize two presentations by Lummi Nation on Labor Day: one for representatives from thirty-two faith communities and another for representatives of forty-four social, environmental, and activist communities. The greater community's response was unprecedented; the groundswell of support was positively overwhelming.

Over the next three years, BUF's partnership with Lummi Nation deepened greatly as BUF sought out every opportunity to support them in the fight against the terminal. From 2013 to 2016, BUF members were invited to support Lummi Nation in putting on a series of annual Totem Pole Journeys to raise awareness and make connections with other nations impacted by the fossil fuels industry. These included the Tsleil-Waututh First Nation near Vancouver, British Columbia, fighting the construction of tar sands pipelines through their lands; the Beaver Lake Cree Nation near Edmonton, Alberta, severely impacted by tar sands extraction; and the Northern Cheyenne in Montana, struggling to save Otter Creek and the Tongue River from being destroyed by coal mining. Each journey helped unite opposition to the fossil fuel export projects and strengthened local, regional, and national networks and alliances.

BUF members also mobilized other Unitarian Universalists to join the struggle, first by helping to initiate a UU College of Social Justice service learning program at Lummi Nation focused on Indigenous history, culture, rights, and intersections with environmental justice. Then, in June 2015, BUF members facilitated a partnership between Lummi Nation and the UUA that resulted in workshops and a public witness event at General Assembly in Portland, Oregon, where Lummi leaders spoke and more than 2,500 people witnessed in solidarity and made spiritual commitments to climate justice. The following year BUF members helped bring the message to the Canadian Unitarian Council General Conference in Vancouver, British Columbia, with a workshop on climate justice, the impact on First Nations, and the imperative of removing human-made borders. Today, BUF members are leading an effort to establish solidarity teams that work locally and regionally with Indigenous nations on their challenges. We hope to start teams in Unitarian Universalist congregations that expand to include members of other faith communities, NGOs, and other concerned citizens.

Partnering with Lummi Nation has been an incredible experience, but that doesn't mean it's been easy. Through past and recent experiences, BUF members have learned that to effectively engage in intersectional justice work with frontline people directly affected by environmental injustice, we have to embrace six key practices: humility, authenticity, listening, cultivating trust, doing our homework, and being in it for the long haul.

PRACTICING HUMILITY

Humility requires that we acknowledge and confront the cultural baggage we bring into any new relationship, and work hard to leave that baggage behind. We all bring assumptions, expectations, and understandings of the way the world works and what's "normal" and valuable that are wrapped up in race, ethnicity, class, age, gender, ability, and more. This baggage is a barrier that must be overcome if we wish to walk in another's world.

For BUF members, practicing humility meant acknowledging and confronting our own racist and ethnocentric tendencies. It also required many of us to let go of an unconscious sense of superiority. We can't ride in on our white horses to "save the Indians" or any other marginalized community. That mentality serves neither them nor us. At times our well-intentioned actions could and did have negative impacts on tribal relations, both within Lummi Nation and in their government-to-government relationships with state and federal entities. Not all tribal members are open to our interference or involvement, and federal and state relationships with the tribe are complex beyond our imagining and understanding. Humility means taking the back seat and allowing their leadership to lead. They know their history and context better than we do and have survived, not because of settlers like us—well-meaning or otherwise—but in spite of us.

We also learned that we had to swallow our sense of pride, become aware of our own egos and be able to set them aside, and acknowledge that we, as non-Indigenous peoples and as members of US culture, often are part of a system that views the Earth as a resource to exploit at any cost, including the exploitation of every being, human and nonhuman. This includes our complicity, our ignorance, and our apathy. As non-Indigenous people it is often tempting to think of ourselves as mere individuals, divorced from our own cultural reality and history, but in fact we have a lot to account for, both in the past and in the present. BUF members also learned that Indigenous cultures have a different relationship to time and ancestry than people who are part of mainstream US culture. To us, the past may seem distant and forgotten; to the Lummi, the past is intertwined with the present, with wounds that run deep and fresh.

BEING AUTHENTIC

Existentialism describes authenticity as the degree to which one is true to one's own personality, spirit, or character, despite external pressures. Showing up and being who you are means letting go of perfectionism or putting up appearances. It also means letting go of motivations like guilt, shame, or pity when it comes to working with marginalized communities.

We've learned that any relationship with frontline communities requires a deep-rooted belief that we have a shared responsibility to preserve the Earth and to honor human rights. It also means being prepared to not only practice what we preach, but to move beyond preaching into substantive action. It means putting ourselves forward as friends and advocates for their sake only, and being careful of taking actions that can be seen as self-serving. We have been cautioned that our zealousness to serve can be interpreted as a boost or balm to our egos, "feigning piety," shaming others who are unable to offer as much, or creating a sense of debt that cannot be repaid. Our actions need to reflect that we have faith in the wisdom of our partners, their leadership, and the causes for which they and we struggle together—not some romantic notion of atonement or other disingenuous ideal. Anything less will be taken as superficial.

LISTENING

The most important skill necessary to effectively engage in cross-cultural partnerships for justice is deep listening. Mainstream US culture greatly values individualism, which means that many of us are primed to value our own interpretations and sense of what's needed or helpful without asking questions, getting into real relationship with one another, or working hard to understand each other's context. We also need to let go of fancy language and speak not from our intellect, but from our heart. Being smart is not the same thing as being wise. At BUF we have needed to hone our skills in listening, interpreting, and translating in order to enter into a First Nations community, where history, time, language, customs, and worldviews are often radically different than ours. For example, we have had to learn the difference between Eagle and eagle, Salmon and salmon, Earth and earth, the People and the people—one is a symbol of Spirit and Culture, the other a name of a mere object. We have needed to be honest and ask clarifying questions when our ignorance has gotten the better of us and accept with grace any admonitions when we've failed to listen and speak accordingly.

CULTIVATING TRUST

Trust is potentially the most vital ingredient in an effective partnership for justice, and it is also one of the most challenging. In order to trust each other, we have to develop real relationships and get to know each other. This process is not quick or easy, especially in cross-cultural situations. It takes time, and it also takes the willingness to get uncomfortable, take risks, own our mistakes, and constantly ask how we can do right by each other. Trust is not something that is granted or built overnight; it is earned over time.

BUF members quickly discovered the importance of trust when working with Lummi members. First Nations peoples have very few reasons to trust settlers and a thousand reasons to distrust them; centuries of broken promises testify to this truth. Cultivating trust with peoples who have experienced centuries of oppression, racism, and both physical and cultural genocide means working through a great deal of sorrow, pain, anger, bitterness, and resentment. Cultivating trust has also meant developing individual relationships between BUF members and Lummi members. There have been times when Unitarian Universalists who are not in personal relationship with Lummi Nation members have expected that they can go into that community to discuss potential collaborations, but just because Lummi members trust particular BUF members doesn't mean they trust all Unitarian Universalists or even all BUF members. Ongoing personal relationships are vital for maintaining trust.

DOING OUR HOMEWORK

Anyone who was raised within mainstream US culture has been taught one-sided views of history and culture—by the media, educational institutions, government, and religious leaders. This means that in cross-cultural relationships one of the most caring things we can do is familiarize ourselves with the cultural context and history of the people with whom we are building a relationship. Find out how you can educate yourself on your own, without depending on a person or group of people to bear the burden of educating you personally. Asking them how you can best educate yourself is a great idea; expecting them to personally educate you can be wearisome at best and insensitive or painful at worst.

For BUF members it was essential to become familiar with First Nations' history, law, and policies, all of which dictate Indigenous peoples' lives in ways we otherwise could not understand. Because mainstream history sources could be negligent and inaccurate, we had to investigate and explore to get a felt sense of things and let our Lummi partners fill in the details from their perspective. BUF members also had to stay open to learning another perspective on history, as well as understand the underbelly of dominant politics and the insidious role that colonization plays in not only destroying the lives and the will of a people, but also its past, present, and future. Members of NACC have not only educated themselves, they have also fostered educational opportunities for others in the congregation, the Whatcom County community, and the Pacific Northwest and beyond.

NACC also had to learn how to respect the relationships and lines of authority within Lummi Nation and other nations. Indigenous nations have complex networks of authority that must be respected in order to stay in right relationship. For example, having a relationship with members of one office or department does not mean you can take that same familiarity into another office or department without consent. And when we were working to organize the public witness event at General Assembly, we had to do our homework to understand relationships between different Indigenous nations and peoples throughout the Pacific Northwest, and how to offer proper respect to different leaders of different Salish Sea Indigenous communities.

BEING IN IT FOR THE LONG HAUL

Many Unitarian Universalist congregations exhibit a "flavor-of-the-day" approach to social justice ministries—either employing numerous different committees, each focused on a different social justice "issue," or quickly jumping from cause to cause. When engaging in cross-cultural partnerships for justice, particularly with oppressed communities, these approaches are completely inappropriate. Long-term commitment is required, as it takes time to build a sense of trust with marginalized peoples and to learn about their histories and challenges.

When it comes to environmental justice, the challenges we face as a species are enormous, complex, and backed by hundreds of years of history, as well as enormous wealth and power. There is no quick fix. Time, effort, and resources are needed to fully understand the social, environmental, economic, and spiritual complexities presented by fossil fuel export terminals, tar sands pipelines, fracking, coal mining, and so on, as well as the impacts on all human and natural communities. More time, effort, and resources will be necessary to craft culturally appropriate responses, alternatives, and solutions, which will be equally as complex.

Commitment is also required to keep fanning the fires when the public's interest wanes or becomes distracted. This became evident in the six years of opposing the proposed coal export terminal, where lulls occurred while waiting on tribal, federal, and state processes to be completed and procedures to be followed. Even the denial of the Corps permit does not secure or protect Xwe'chi'eXen from court appeals or other development projects. Environmental injustices are well entrenched in US law, politics, and economics. These arenas are slow in changing and need persistent prodding in order to effect the necessary changes. We must be committed to the hard work it takes to undo the injustice built into our society while simultaneously practicing vigilance to prevent future injustices.

The partnership with Lummi Nation has had a transformative impact on BUF. Ten years ago, our congregation saw social justice as an individual endeavor, not a congregational one. Though members were connected to myriad social justice opportunities in the wider community, we were not a "social justice congregation." Our partnership with Lummi Nation changed that. In 2013, BUF passed a congregational resolution to support Lummi Nation in protecting Xwe'chi'eXen. This decision—to perform social justice work on a congregational level by engaging the entire congregation in support of Lummi Nation—was a difficult one for some people. It challenged us to become a whole body involved in social justice and band together with a common purpose. Some people resisted this change, and we even lost members over it. However, not only have we gained far more members than we lost, we have also gained so much more. Now, people who come through BUF's doors for community environmental and social justice events come back on Sunday morning for worship services, and some of them have signed the membership book. They love the fact that BUF now sees itself as an active participant in social change. But more than that, BUF has gained incredible connections to our wider community, to other Unitarian Universalist congregations, and to environmental and social justice organizations and networks throughout the Pacific Northwest and beyond. In 2015 BUF organized local congregations to petition the UUA Pacific Northwest District to sign an interfaith statement of solidarity with native peoples to safeguard their traditional lands, waters, and sacred sites from destruction. Since then, we have been building powerful relationships with three regional and state action networks— the Northwest UU Justice Network, Washington State UU Voices for Justice, and Oregon UU Voices for Justice. BUF was particularly proud to host the Northwest UU Justice Network's annual summit in 2015, where representatives from congregations throughout the Pacific Northwest came together. BUF is not isolated anymore; we are part of a larger network of people working for justice.

Because there were a few dedicated people within the Bellingham Unitarian Fellowship and Lummi Nation willing to make the commitment, build the trust, and work together to build the necessary bridges, we have reached and are continuing to engage people of conscience throughout North America and beyond. We are a part of a larger movement that is shifting the consciousness of the peoples on this planet not only in terms of confronting environmental and climate justice and following the leadership of frontlines people in the struggle, but also in raising the awareness that no matter our race, culture, or species, we all have a shared responsibility and a sacred obligation to honor each other and preserve the Earth for all her children.

> The Earth does not belong to us. We belong to
>   the Earth.
> Whatever befalls the Earth
> befalls the sons and daughters of the Earth.
> We did not weave the web of life,
> we are merely strands in it.
> Whatever we do to that web, we do to
>   ourselves.
> > —attributed to Si'ahl (Seattle), hereditary
> > chief of the Suquamish and Duwamish
> > Nations in the Pacific Northwest

TAKING IT FURTHER

Deb Cruz and Alex Kapitan note the tendency of religious communities to scatter their justice-related energies among a wide range of disparate causes or jump from cause to cause, depending on what's currently in the news. Is your community committed for the long haul to a specific cause or an affected group of people? If so, how did your community arrive at that depth of engagement? What was the history and process? If not, are there structural or other barriers that are preventing your community from realizing a depth of engagement?

. . . . .

Is your religious community engaged in ongoing multicultural collaboration? How might you collectively deepen your skills, either in the midst of such collaboration or in readiness for such collaboration? Take a look at the following resource, and see how it might support your efforts: https://tinyurl.com/yb2sz4gw.

. . . . .

How would a deeper awareness of yourself and the way that you understand the world help you practice humility in a cross-cultural relationship? How do you, and how do we collectively, respond when confronted with worldviews and life experiences that challenge our personal understandings?

Concluding Reflections

MANISH MISHRA–MARZETTI

Recognizing that a problem exists and doing something concrete about it can be two entirely different propositions. In spiritual circles, it is sometimes said that the biggest step one can take is from one's head to one's heart. In a similar manner, when it comes to justice-making, the biggest and most important step may be moving from one's head to embodied action. We cannot always "think" our way into a more just world, but we sure can think our way out of it, in any number of ways. As we conclude our reflections on environmental justice and intersectional justice-making, I'd like to explore some of the "thoughts" that can stifle our justice-making potential.

"The problem is HUGE, what difference can I possibly make? And, to boot, my heart and head are in the right place. I'm not part of the problem." This line of thinking, sometimes explicitly articulated but often quietly held, immobilizes us. We assume that our intellectual and moral commitment places us in the box of "those who are good on this issue" without needing to take any further responsibility or concrete action. This impulse is then reinforced by the idea that whatever problem we are looking at is so intractable, so large, so complicated, so systemic, that there is nothing any one person could do to change the overall dynamics.

There is some grain of truth in this latter idea. As this book seeks to underscore, deeply rooted social problems are intersectional and systemic; this is exactly why many of the socioeconomic-environmental issues discussed here are of a persistent and viciously reinforcing nature. The complex, deeply intertwined nature of the challenges at hand may require a mode of response that is just as deeply intersectional.

I consider myself a lifelong justice activist. Like many religious progressives, social injustice has never sat well with me, and I have long done whatever I can to work for a world in which the human dignity of all is held in regard. As I look back at my decades of justice activism, I can clearly see how siloed and issue-specific my activism has been: gay/lesbian-focused, race-focused, and transgender equality-focused. Yes, allies are always brought into this work from a broad spectrum of backgrounds, but the galvanizing energy has almost always been focused on a single issue. This silo effect unintentionally separates justice advocates from one another. Those with a passion for the environment may not see or believe that their issue intersects with race; those with a passion for gay/lesbian rights may not see how their commitments intersect with issues of endemic poverty; those with a passion for education or affordable housing may not see the ways in which their cause connects with issues of nutrition and food security, and so on. We do the good work that we are doing, somewhat removed from others who are just as passionate as us but about different issues, believing perhaps that if those other folk "saw the light" they would care about our issue as much as they care about their own.

This silo effect has one well-proven result: It keeps entrenched, systemic problems in place. Our separation from one another as justice advocates allows the largest, most thorny intersectional problems to remain largely intact, as issue-focused groups chew on different, limited slices of whatever is going on. We need to bring a power analysis to bear on this, and realize that we are much larger and stronger working together, from the lens of intersectionality, than we are from issue-driven silos. This possibility invites us to be intentional about seeking out and meeting one another at the inter-sections, building shared agendas from there. The Unitarian Universalist Ministry for Earth (UUMFE) recognized this, expending organizational time and financial resources explic-itly for the purpose of pulling together the 2014 Detroit Col-laboratory, an intentionally intersectional gathering of disparate justice activists.

"But what about my problem? Sure, there are people suf-fering in the world, but my life isn't a cakewalk either." The impulse toward justice is often stymied by the nagging inter-nal recognition that "I have problems, too." Sometimes this comes from a place of pain—the impact of seeing and feeling the attention of others, maybe even the world, on a given prob-lem, while holding a sense of private struggle over whatever it may be that one is personally navigating. This can lead to unexpressed resentment and the feeling that one's own pain or personal issues are just as important as whatever set of issues someone else is struggling with: We arrive at an often subconscious moral equivalency. This kind of thinking also serves to keep us in the realm of the intellect, as opposed to action: "We human beings all suffer in different ways, and unlike others in the world, my beliefs, understandings, and heart are all in the right place." Holding this intellectual commitment can become all that we do.

It is both human and natural to notice and care about our own struggles. A dozen years out of seminary, I personally hold so much student debt that I feel, at times, like I'm an indentured laborer for the bank. I have no secure possibility of retirement in my future, and no idea how I'll save enough money for the education of my own children. It is both natural and easy to get caught up in all of this, or any other number of possibilities: personal health challenges, the need to care for aging parents, or vocational uncertainty. The list of personal cares and preoccupations is potentially endless. And yet, I did not grow up next to, nor do I currently live adjacent to, a trash dump. I have always been able to turn on the tap water and safely drink what comes out. I never went to elementary school breathing in the fumes of the incinerator next door. This is the fundamental, lived reality of many poorer communities of color in the United States today, and it is a deliberate political outcome, shaped by decades of policy, for the benefit of those who have greater financial resources and political influence. This is the very definition of selfishness, and as people of faith we are called to step into a greater and wider sense of shared humanity.

"What about the starving children in India? They have it much worse." This may, in fact, be true. And, we could easily substitute "India" with any number of countries—Afghanistan, Ghana, the Dominican Republic, you name it. There is a long list of places on the planet where human beings may be living with objectively less wealth, less access to clean water, and greater hardship all around. My observation as a spiritual leader is that this objectively greater level of hardship and suffering in other countries is easier for religious progressives to step into than the hardship and suffering that is closer to home. There are several reasons for this. Stepping into the inequality and suffering we have created in our own nation requires explicitly or implicitly beginning to recognize our complicity and silence in allowing that suffering to exist: We must contend with conscious or subconscious guilt and denial. As a moral commitment, financially or otherwise supporting starving children in India is absolutely a good thing to do. We get to check off the mental "I am a good person" box without necessarily digging deeper into how the middle-class comfort we may enjoy in our own nation is shaped and on whose backs it exists.

We can and should support whatever good we can do in the broader global context. However, if we are only doing that without digging deeply into the domestic social inequities of which we are a part, we are engaging in denial, pure and simple. We are left with a choice. We can either remain a witting or unwitting accomplice to deeply entrenched, mutually

reinforcing patterns of poverty and oppression that predominantly affect people of color in our nation, or we can wake
up to these realities and become a part of the systemic change
that is needed. As an Indo-American, I'm grateful for whatever we can do to help starving children in India, but we
Americans are the only ones who can fix our own broken-
ness. No one else is going to do that for us.

Our intention for this book is that it serve as a resource
in helping individuals and communities think about and
practice engaging in the work of intersectional justice-
making. In addition, I hope that we've also delivered a challenge. The issues that we face as a nation today are just as great
as what we confronted in the 1950s and 1960s. At that time,
we had to go deep within ourselves to see how we were com-
plicit with structures of power, authority, and organization
that were abusive and harmful. Collectively, as a nation, we
responded to that challenge and made large-scale, systemic
changes that moved us toward being a better nation. We have
tackled similarly entrenched problems before, and with courage and conviction we must do so again. Our spiritual commitment to human dignity and equality demands nothing
less of us.

JENNIFER NORDSTROM

I hold a vision of Beloved Community beyond the horizon
of my own knowing. In this community of human and
nonhuman beings, we live in integrity with each other and

the Earth. We work together to nourish and sustain life. We eat well, but do not take more than we need from each other or the Earth. We have diverse, flourishing cultures that cooperate with, respect, and learn from one another without prejudice or hierarchy. We live free from violence and coercion. We celebrate every day, and appreciate the joys of living. We dance and sing. We laugh. While we help one another die well, we do not help death come before its time. We use our minds to the benefit of life, not death. We create art and music. We tell stories. We live in tune with the rhythms of the Earth: the seasons, day and night. We live in tune with each other. We live in tune with the rhythms of our own hearts.

I don't know how to get there, but I know the first few moves in that direction. And I have faith that we will discover the next moves after we make the first ones. First, we must build communities that are spiritually and relationally resilient so we have the strength to resist the painful patterns of power and oppression in which we currently live. We must resist the death structures of capitalism, white supremacy, and patriarchy, and create communities that will nourish our souls as we do so. We must also simultaneously build the alternatives to those structures. We must begin building the capacity to live differently. There are thousands of beginnings to living differently, and each one must come from specific local needs. In this book, we have shared some examples of how various communities are building resilience and movements for resistance. We have shared examples of communities that have analyzed their local contexts and identified first moves on the path to living differently. These stories are examples within the frame of environmental justice. We must hold the big vision, the one just beyond the horizon, of Beloved Community of humanity and nonhuman beings living in harmony with each other and the Earth, and begin to move toward it today, in our specific place, time, and community.

References

Rita Nakashima Brock and Rebecca Ann Parker, *Saving Paradise: How Christianity Traded Love of This World for Crucifixion and Empire.* Boston: Beacon Press, 2009.

Walter Brueggemann, *The Prophetic Imagination.* Minneapolis: Fortress Press, 2001.

Robert Bullard, "Solid Waste Sites and the Black Houston Community," *Sociological Inquiry,* Volume 53, Issue 2–3, April 1983.

Karen Baker-Fletcher, *Sisters of Dust, Sisters of Spirit: Womanist Wordings on God and Creation.* Minneapolis: Augsburg-Fortress Press, 1998.

Hosea Ballou, *An Examination of the Doctrine of Future Retribution: On the Principles of Morals, Analogy and the Scriptures.* Boston: Trumpet Office, 1834.

Joshua Bloom and Waldo E. Martin, Jr., *Black against Empire: The History and Politics of the Black Panther Party.* Berkeley: University of California Press, 2013.

The Commission on Appraisal, *Engaging Our Theological Diversity.* Boston: UUA, 2005.

James H. Cone, "Whose Earth Is it Anyway?" *Sojourners,* July 2007.

Gopal Dayaneni, "Resilience-Based Organizing": http://movementgeneration.org/our-work/movementbuilding-2/resiliencebasedorganizing.

John Dickson, "Fossil Fuel," *Poetry*, October 1985.

Alison Downie, "A Spirituality of Openness: Christian Ecofeminist Perspectives and Inter-religious Dialogue" in *Feminist Theology*, Volume 23, Issue 1, September 2014.

Elk River Blues, documentary film: https://vimeo.com/ 117438040.

Ralph Waldo Emerson, "Nature" in *Essays and Lectures*. New York: Library of America, 1983.

Sarah Frostenson and Sarah Kliff, "Where is the lead exposure risk in your community?" vox.com, April 6, 2016.

Ivone Gebara, *Longing for Running Water: Ecofeminism and Liberation*. Minneapolis: Fortress Press, 1999.

Linda Gerstein, *Dust Bowl Meets Great Depression: Environmental Tools & Tales of the Dust Bowl*, B.A. thesis: http://hdl.handle.net/ 10066/6694.

Barbara Holmes, *Race and the Cosmos: An Invitation to View the World Differently*. Bloomsbury, United Kingdom: Bloomsbury, 2002.

Debby Irving, *Waking Up White and Finding Myself in the Story of Race*. Cambridge, MA: Elephant Room Press, 2014.

Fredric Jameson, *The Seeds of Time*. New York: Columbia University Press, 1994.

Fredric Jameson, "Future City," *New Left Review* 21, May/June 2003.

Kabir, *Kabir: Ecstatic Poems*. Robert Bly, trans. Boston: Beacon Press, 2004.

Catherine Keller, *The Face of the Deep: A Theology of Becoming*. New York: Routledge Press, 2002.

Naomi Klein, *This Changes Everything: Capitalism vs. the Climate*. New York: Simon & Schuster, 2014.

Aldo Leopold, *A Sand County Almanac with Essays on Conservation from Round River*. New York: Ballantine Books, 1966.

Sallie McFague, *The Body of God: An Ecological Theology*. Minneapolis: Fortress Press, 1993.

Paul Outka, *Race and Nature from Transcendentalism to the Harlem Renaissance*. New York: Palgrave Macmillan, 2008.

Bill Plotkin, *Nature and the Human Soul: Cultivating Wholeness and Community in a Fragmented World*. Novato, CA: New World Library, 2008.

Doyle Rice, "Rain that caused deadly Md. flood a '1-in-1,000' year event," *USA Today*, August 1, 2016.

Shamara Shantu Riley, "Ecology Is a Sistah's Issue Too," in *This Sacred Earth: Religion, Nature, Environment*, ed. Roger S. Gottlieb. New York: Taylor & Francis Books, 2004.

Mayra Rivera, *The Touch of Transcendence: A Postcolonial Theology of God*. Louisville, KY: Westminster John Knox Press, 2007.

Rosemary Radford Ruether, *Gaia & God: An Ecofeminist Theology of Earth Healing*. New York: HarperOne, 1992.

Lynn White, Jr., "The Historical Roots of Our Ecologic Crisis," *Science* 155, No. 3767, Mar. 10, 1967.

About the Contributors

SOFIA BETANCOURT is a Unitarian Universalist minister who serves as assistant professor of Unitarian Universalist theologies and ethics at Starr King School for the Ministry and is a Ph.D. candidate at Yale University in the Department of Religious Ethics and African American Studies. She served for four years as the director of racial and ethnic concerns of the Unitarian Universalist Association, and from April to June of 2017, she served as interim co-president of the UUA for the Commission on Institutional Change. She was the first woman and the first woman of color to serve as UUA president.

PEGGY CLARKE is the minister at the First Unitarian of Westchester in Hastings-on-Hudson, New York. She serves on the executive committees for the UU-UNO Climate Justice Initiative, Commit2Respond, and the UU Environmental Justice Collaboratory, and she chaired the UU Food Justice Ministry for five years. She was a chaplain at Iona College, where she also served as adjunct professor in the Religious Studies Department and co-directed the Iona Spirituality Institute. She is an activist, a GreenFaith Fellow, and the co-founder of InterGenerate, an organization dedicated to food justice.

DEBORAH J. CRUZ is a member of the Bellingham Unitarian Fellowship (BUF) in Bellingham, Washington. She co-chaired BUF's Green Sanctuary Program and is chair of the Climate Justice and co-chair of the Native American Connections ministry teams. She is also a board member of the Northwest UU Justice Network. She has been involved with First Nations issues since the mid-1970s, including working with Lummi Nation in opposition to the Gateway Pacific Terminal proposed for development on their sacred lands and waters of Cherry Point.

ROSE EDINGTON and **MEL HOOVER** are co-ministers emeriti of the Unitarian Universalist Congregation in Charleston, West Virginia. To carry their activism into retirement, they founded MelRose Ministries for Positive Transformative Change. Earlier in his career, Mel served on the staff of the Unitarian Universalist Association, where he directed its national justice work, overseeing the anitiracism, anti-oppression, and multicultural ministries programs. He also served on President Bill Clinton's One America Task Force. In 2013, he received the UUA's Annual Award for Distinguished Service. He is on the board of UU Ministry for Earth. Rose is on the board of the Ohio Valley Environmental Coalition, where she has also served as its president and is the recipient of its outstanding volunteer of the year award. Both Mel and Rose are members of the steering committee for West Virginia Interfaith Power and Light.

PAULA COLE JONES is a management consultant, specializing in group facilitation, diversity, and social justice. She also worked as a natural resource manager with the U.S. Department of Agriculture, and as an environmental specialist with the District of Columbia government. She is the founder of A Dialogue On Race & Ethnicity (ADORE), and the editor of *Encounters: Poems about Race, Ethnicity and Identity*, published by Skinner House Books.

ALEX KAPITAN is an anti-oppression activist, organizer, educator, writer, and editor. Founder of the project Radical Copyeditor and co-leader of the Transforming Hearts Collective, Alex helps people of faith practice radical inclusion, does interfaith work to help queer and trans folk connect to religion and spirituality, and also does social justice-informed writing and editing. Find out more at www.radicalcopyeditor.com and www.transformingheartscollective.org.

MATTHEW McHALE is an environmental/climate justice and racial justice activist. He has served on the steering committees of the UU Environmental Justice Collaboratory, UU Young Adults for Climate Justice, and Allies for Racial Equity. He is a proponent of cooperative living and permaculture, and first got involved in resilience-based organizing with Occupy the Farm in Berkeley, California. He serves as the minister at Emerson Unitarian Universalist Church in Los Angeles.

KATHLEEN McTIGUE is the director of the Unitarian Universalist College of Social Justice, a program developed and supported jointly by the UUA and the UUSC. Prior to assuming this role in 2012, she served as a parish minister for twenty-one years in New Haven, Connecticut, and for four years in Winston-Salem, North Carolina. She is married to community organizer Nick Nyhart; they have three adult children.

MANISH MISHRA-MARZETTI serves as senior minister of The First Parish in Lincoln, Massachusetts, a dual UUA and United Church of Christ member congregation. He has served extensively in UU leadership, including as president of the Diverse and Revolutionary Unitarian Universalist Multicultural Ministries (a people of color organization), and currently as a trustee on the UUA Board of Trustees. Prior to entering the ministry, he was a US diplomat during the Clinton Administration. He loves desert hiking and his amazing kids and husband.

JENNIFER NORDSTROM is the senior minister of the First Unitarian Society of Milwaukee. The founder of the Unitarian Universalist Young Adults for Climate Justice, she is deeply committed to co-creating faith-based movements for climate and environmental justice. Prior to ministry, Jennifer organized for social justice at the intersections of gender, class, race, nationality, militarism, and the environment. She believes Unitarian Universalism can help build the Beloved Community.

SHERI PRUD'HOMME is the minister for faith development at the First Unitarian Church of Oakland. Her Ph.D. dissertation, completed in 2016, focused on Thomas Starr King's theology of nature in his Yosemite and Sierra Nevada sermons. She also has an article, "Emerson's Hermeneutic of the Text of Moral Nature," in the *American Journal of Theology and Philosophy*, September 2014. She is an avid hiker, educator, and mother of two proud Unitarian Universalists.

ADAM ROBERSMITH is a Unitarian Universalist minister and spiritual director, serving the Universalist Church of West Hartford, Connecticut. His academic and ministerial work focuses on spiritual formation in Unitarian Universalist and other liberal religious communities. Outside of ministry, he is a gardener, hiker, aspiring permaculturist, and a believer in the interdependent web of all existence as an embodiment of Universalism.

PAMELA SPARR has a passion for promoting spiritually-grounded, intersectional activism. Personally, and through her professional career, she has advanced environmental and climate justice at local, national, and international levels by offering popular education for adults and youth, facilitating solidarity actions with frontline communities, and engaging in the nuts and bolts of policy formulation and advocacy. A Unitarian Universalist, she helped strengthen the environmental justice components of the UUA's Green Sanctuary program and pass the UU Statement of Conscience on climate change.